PATHWISE®
FRAMEWORK COMPONENT
MINICOURSES FOR TEACHERS

DEMONSTRATING
KNOWLEDGE OF STUDENTS

ACKNOWLEDGMENTS

I wish to thank the staff at ETS for the opportunity to work on this minicourse. In addition, Annette Parks, Pennie Pine, and Gayla Moilanen helped me by providing suggestions. I also want to extend special thanks to Amanda McBride and Salli Long for their significant contributions to the content and structure of the workbook.

Educational Testing Service
Teaching and Learning Division

Educational Testing Service
MS 18-D
Rosedale Road
Princeton, NJ 08541-0001
Web site: http://www.ets.org/pathwise

ISBN 0-88686-233-1

Printed in the United States of America

07 06 05 04 03 02   10 9 8 7 6 5 4 3 2 1

CONTENTS

PREFACE

An Introduction for Administrators: PATHWISE Minicourses for Teachers. v
To Teachers: Before You Begin vi
Standards of Professional Practice. viii
The Minicourse Learning Cycle ix
About Related Activities xi

PART I: UNDERSTANDING THE VALUE OF DEVELOPING A DEEP
KNOWLEDGE OF YOUR STUDENTS

Getting to Know Your Students. 1
How Student Motivation and Engagement Influence Learning. 4
Factors That Influence Student Engagement and Motivation. 6
How Knowledge of Students Can Help You Engage and Motivate
    Your Students 8
Why Do I Need This Information?. 10
A Level-of-Performance Scale 12
Related Activities 16

PART II: BUILDING DEEPER KNOWLEDGE OF STUDENTS

Developing Your Knowledge Base 25
The Tools of Your Investigation 28
    Organizational Models 29
    Investigative Methods 51
The Investigative Process for Building Knowledge of Students 64
Related Activities 68

PART III: USING KNOWLEDGE OF STUDENTS TO ENHANCE
INSTRUCTIONAL PRACTICE

Filtering Through Gathered Information 89
Thinking About Your Own Teaching Style. 91
Considerations for Using Knowledge of Your Students to
    Inform Your Practice 92
Gathering Ideas for New Teaching Strategies 93
Using Knowledge of Students to Develop a Student-Focused
    Approach to Teaching. 93
Differentiated Instruction. 94
Group Learning. 103
Assessment 107
Collecting and Evaluating What You Have Learned 111
Related Activities 114

PART IV: DEEPENING AND APPLYING YOUR KNOWLEDGE OF STUDENTS

Thinking About Knowledge of Students as it Applies to Teaching 125
The Investigative Process for Building Knowledge of Students 128
The Investigative Process for Building Knowledge of Students—A Review . . . 130
Related Activities 139

PART V: REFLECTING, ASSESSING, AND PLANNING FUTURE ADVANCEMENT

Your Continuing Progress 145
Reflecting on Your Accomplishments 147
Making a Connection—Checkpoints 148
Self-Assessing Your Current Proficiency 154
Planning Future Advancement 156
Related Activities 158

APPENDICES

Appendix A: A Framework for Teaching 166
Appendix B: Resources 168
Appendix C: Selected References 177
Appendix D: Related Activities Completion Charts 183

PATHWISE® Minicourses for Teachers

The Teaching and Learning Division of Educational Testing Service (ETS®) has developed a series of minicourses to support the growing number of teaching professionals who are engaged in continuous inquiry on their own or through school-level, peer-supported, self-directed professional development programs, such as the PATHWISE®: Framework Portfolio Program.

PATHWISE Minicourses are research-based, skill-specific guides to improving key components of professional teaching practice. They are designed to be used by individual teachers or by teachers working collaboratively. While the framework of the minicourses supports processes explored in the Portfolio Program, it is not necessary to know or use the Portfolio Program to benefit from the minicourses.

PATHWISE Minicourses provide teachers with a powerful, structured, self-directed approach to systematically and comprehensively examine, critique, and improve particular elements of individual teaching practice.

Each minicourse:

- **situates** a particular classroom skill in the overall practice of teaching

- **describes** the value of the skill in terms of enhancing student learning

- **provides** a level-of-performance scale for assessing the skill

- **points** to resources that particularize the skill

- **provides** valuable information about using the skill in the classroom

- **offers** opportunities for self-reflection on current skill levels

- **guides** teachers in a step-by-step approach to setting goals for advancing proficiency

- **provides** practical tools and advice for improving a skill incrementally in the classroom

- **encourages** ongoing reflection, with the goal of continuously enriching student learning

All PATHWISE Minicourses are grounded in established professional standards for teaching. They are intended to help individual teachers—and groups of teachers working together—structure their own, self-directed learning, apply this new learning in the classroom, and use student learning as evidence of their growing effectiveness.

PATHWISE Minicourse workbooks are designed to help teachers identify areas for professional growth and to practice their skills in a continuous learning cycle. Teachers use the minicourses to set their own professional goals and to guide themselves in developing and implementing plans to achieve them. One minicourse may be reused several times as teachers continuously and incrementally refine their skills.

TO TEACHERS:
BEFORE YOU BEGIN ...

This PATHWISE Minicourse is designed to help you — a teaching professional interested in advancing your own practice — refine a key professional skill: developing a deeper, more substantive knowledge of your students so that you can better plan instructional and assessment strategies to support student engagement, student thinking, and student learning. Research shows that teachers who know their students are better able to differentiate instruction to allow students to work to their strengths while learning new things. Yet, most of what teachers have learned about getting to know their students and the value of this information has been learned on the job. It's not the kind of information that is typically presented in school, at in-service workshops, or during informal talks with colleagues. This minicourse has been designed to address this void by providing teachers with a systematic approach for collecting and interpreting information about their students (that is, getting to know their students) and using that information to set goals, plan lessons, and select and modify instructional and assessment strategies.

This minicourse provides information integrated with activities that move in a stepwise fashion toward the application of your newfound knowledge of your students as you plan a lesson or unit and create a classroom atmosphere that inspires learning and accepts and holds high expectations for all students. The workbook is organized around the PATHWISE Minicourse Learning Cycle, which can be repeated multiple times as you incrementally advance your teaching practice. Related Activities, provided at the end of each unit, are designed to help you gather information about your students so that you can more effectively teach them. These activities also require you to reflect on your current teaching practice and set your own goals for increasing your knowledge of your students.

PART I — Understanding the Value of Developing a Deep Knowledge of Your Students

Students are wonderfully complex, ever-changing individuals, each with a unique way of seeing, experiencing, and responding to the world around them. They come to our classrooms prepackaged, with their own individual learning styles and preferences, family and cultural backgrounds, interests, passions, skills, abilities, gifts, talents, and (of course) needs. Their individuality and mutability can be at once exciting and challenging for those who are responsible for guiding them toward deeper, more meaningful learning. Understanding and responding to these differences enhance your ability to select and shape instruction and assessment techniques to support and motivate student learning. Part I of this minicourse elaborates on the various elements that comprise "Knowledge of Students," explains the types of information teachers should try to collect as they go about the process of developing a deeper knowledge of their students, discusses how this information can be used to design more meaningful instructional and assessment strategies, and describes proficiency in this area. Related Activities in Part I ask you to examine your current knowledge of the students you are teaching and to consider how you are applying that knowledge to your teaching. You are also asked to select at least two students, who you will use as focal points of your learning and investigation throughout this minicourse. Journal space is provided to help direct your reflection and organize your thoughts.

PART II — Building Deeper Knowledge of Students

Central to the idea of a student-focused approach to learning is the notion that every student is entitled to have a chance to achieve his or her full learning potential. Developing a deep, sensitive knowledge of students is an essential part of ensuring that that each student has that opportunity. Part II examines the types of information you can gather about your students, helps you to determine what information will be helpful to you, and provides examples of how to go about obtaining that information. The Related Activities at the end of the unit are designed to help you evaluate your current methods for getting to know your students and to develop additional techniques. You begin to gather information about the two students selected for focus at this time.

PART III — Using Knowledge of Students to Enhance Instructional Practice

After you have built a more thorough understanding of the many different ways you can "know your students" and the various tools of the trade for developing that knowledge, you are ready to learn how you can apply what you have learned about your students to your practice. Part III shows you how you might adjust your instructional approaches to respond to the learning needs of your students. At this time, you will begin to consider what steps you would like to take to improve your own skills in support of this teaching proficiency.

PART IV   Deepening and Applying Your Knowledge of Students

Part IV guides you, step by step, through the process of interpreting and applying knowledge of students using information collected up to this point. Related Activities in this section are intended to help you complete and implement a plan for applying skills and knowledge you've developed about your students to your practice.

PART V   Reflecting, Assessing, and Planning Future Advancement

The final section of this minicourse is more about beginnings than endings. In Part V, you look back on the thoughtful steps you have taken to develop a deeper knowledge of your students (and as a result, enhance their learning). You also begin to plan for the future—toward the next steps you plan to make on your road to developing more insightful, respectful, instructive knowledge of your students. Related Activities in Part V guide you in a constructive assessment of what you and your students have done differently and whether or not these changes have been advantageous. This assessment doubles as the initial plan for your next incremental advancement.

As you move through this minicourse, take time to get to know your students and reflect upon how important this knowledge is for your own growth as a teacher. It is important to do this thoughtfully and systematically, and to allow yourself ample time to learn about your students and apply that knowledge. It will take time to restructure the way you teach, and it is unreasonable to think you can change your goals and your instructional and assessment methods to meet every child's needs. But the changes you do make will leave a lasting impression on your students. They will appreciate your taking time to learn more about them and making adjustments in your instruction to meet their individual needs—and, more than likely, will respond with new enthusiasm, diligence, and motivation. Make these changes incrementally, with a clear focus on your lesson goals and the standards upon which they are based.

STANDARDS OF PROFESSIONAL PRACTICE

A set of professional standards provides a common language for talking about teaching. PATHWISE Minicourses rely on the components of good teaching described in *Enhancing Professional Practice: A Framework for Teaching* by Charlotte Danielson.[1] These professional standards are aligned to the principles of the Interstate New Teacher Assessment and Support Consortium, as well as other standards for teachers.

---

[1] Danielson, C. (1996). *Enhancing professional practice: A framework for teaching.* Alexandria, VA: Association for Supervision and Curriculum Development. Available: http://shop.ascd.org (search by title from this Web page).

In her book, Danielson divides instructional practice into four principal domains with 22 related components. Within this framework, "Demonstrating Knowledge of Students" is a component of Domain 1: Planning and Preparation. (To examine a graphic that shows how this component is situated within the larger framework of teaching, see Appendix A.)

THE MINICOURSE LEARNING CYCLE

All PATHWISE Minicourses are organized around a learning cycle that can be repeated as you incrementally advance your teaching practice. In Part I of the minicourse—the first stage of the cycle—you gather and reflect on new information pertinent to this particular area of professional development, and begin to self-assess your practice with respect to this skill area. In Part II, after deeper consideration of the skill under discussion (in this case, developing a more substantive level of knowledge about the students you teach and applying that knowledge to instruction), you reflect more specifically on your current teaching practice with regard to this skill, and you set an incremental learning goal to further your development. In Part III, the third stage of the minicourse cycle, you examine related issues that support the skill and reflect on ways these issues may affect your success as well as student learning. In Part IV, you plan and implement information-gathering techniques and profile-building skills to help you gain a deeper understanding of your students, and begin to plan what type of evidence you will need to collect (and how you can collect it) in order to assess your success in this skill. Finally, in Part V, you reflect on your new learning and answer questions that may later form the basis of your next incremental advancement.

Point of clarification: The PATHWISE Minicourse Learning Cycle, as has been explained, is the learning cycle you follow to advance your own professional development. Later, in Part II of this minicourse, you will also be introduced to an Investigative Process for Building Knowledge About Your Students. This is a process you will use as you go about developing your knowledge of your students. In other words, the PATHWISE Minicourse Learning Cycle guides your learning with respect to your own professional development; the Investigative Process is a method you can use when applying this new skill to deepen your knowledge of the students you teach.

THE PATHWISE MINICOURSE LEARNING CYCLE

STAGE I
Gather and reflect on new information; begin to self-assess your practice.

STAGE II
Consider the skill more deeply; identify knowledge you want to integrate into your practice; set an incremental learning goal.

STAGE V
Reflect on your new learning; take notes that form the basis of your next incremental advancement.

STAGE III
Examine related issues that support the skill; prepare students for the new approach you will use with them.

STAGE IV
Plan and implement the investigative process in which you rehearse the skill at a new level.

This learning cycle is supported by a series of Related Activities that are provided at the end of each chapter in the PATHWISE Minicourse workbook. These activities are intended to help you identify areas for professional growth and to practice your skills in a continuous learning cycle.

About Related Activities

The Related Activities in this minicourse provide tools to help you gather information about your students so that you can better understand them, and use this new understanding to enhance your instructional and assessment practices. Your completion of these activities should reflect your own learning style and current level of proficiency. It is not essential to use complete sentences when working on these activities; bulleted lists or numbered phrases may be more helpful to you. However, it is important to document your thoughts and your progress. This documentation can serve as an invaluable resource to you as you revisit topics and pursue deeper levels of understanding and application.

NOTES

PART I

OBJECTIVES:

- UNDERSTAND THE FOUR ELEMENTS THAT COMPRISE THE "KNOWLEDGE OF STUDENTS" FRAMEWORK COMPONENT.

- UNDERSTAND HOW KNOWLEDGE OF STUDENTS ENHANCES INSTRUCTION AND, AS A RESULT, BENEFITS STUDENT LEARNING.

- BECOME FAMILIAR WITH THE LEVEL-OF-PERFORMANCE SCALE.

GETTING TO KNOW YOUR STUDENTS

There is a great deal more to good teaching than being well versed in a subject and its related pedagogy. The most effective teachers are also skilled practitioners of the art of getting to know their students and applying that knowledge in ways that help those students become more successful learners. Taking the time to get to know as much as possible about your students—their interests, talents, strengths, concerns, and learning styles, as well as cultural, social, and family influences—helps you plan effective, meaningful lessons that engage and challenge your students, and gives you the information you need to assess your students' learning more accurately and in ways that will inform your teaching. In so doing, you will be able to plan instruction and assessment that will challenge your students without overwhelming and frustrating them—and, as a result, you will help your students feel more confident in their own learning abilities and therefore more excited about and motivated to learn.

In the teaching framework upon which this and other PATHWISE Minicourses are based, the "Demonstrating Knowledge of Students" component is comprised of four elements:

CHARACTERISTICS OF AGE GROUP

Each age group has certain developmental characteristics—intellectual, social, physical, and emotional. Teachers need to be familiar with these characteristics so that they can recognize when students' behavior or learning progress is out of sync with what would be expected for children their age; and they need to be able to apply this understanding to instruction. For example, fifth-grade teachers know what is developmentally appropriate for 10-year-olds, and how children in this age group are likely to react in various situations. They know the areas of growth that can be expected during the school year and the range of expected behaviors and levels of understanding. For this reason, they are also able to determine when a student is not achieving those usual expectations, and they can adjust their instructional and assessment strategies accordingly. They also communicate their observations (and explain how they are responding to these observations) to the students' families. When necessary, they seek the assistance of other school professionals — for further information that may explain or clarify their observations, as well as guidance in how to respond to these observations.

STUDENTS' VARIED APPROACHES TO LEARNING

Students vary enormously in how they process information, as well as how they most comfortably and successfully approach learning. For example, some students learn better by reading, others through studying images, others by listening, and still others through hands-on experience; some prefer working alone while others learn better when interacting with others; and some require calm, quiet surroundings while others thrive on high-energy environments filled with music, posters, and light. Teachers need to understand and recognize these different approaches to learning and be able to incorporate a range of instructional strategies to support them to help students meet or exceed content standards.

STUDENTS' SKILLS AND KNOWLEDGE

Because learning is an ongoing process that builds on previous knowledge and skills, students are able to understand new information best when it is based on accurate prior knowledge.

Students bring an extensive range of skills, interests, and knowledge with them to the classroom. These include academic knowledge as well as out-of-school knowledge of everyday events, topics of interest, and activities. Because students are actively constructing meaning, they build their new understandings on what they already know. Skilled teachers are able to identify these areas of prior knowledge, and they are able to use this information to design instructional strategies that build on what their students already know and can do.

Because learning is an ongoing process that builds on previous knowledge and skills, students are able to understand new information best when it is based on accurate prior knowledge. But, for many reasons, students sometimes develop and hold onto misconceptions or misunderstandings that can interfere with their learning. Teachers need to be able to identify these misconceptions, and they should be familiar with areas of misunderstandings that are common for students in the grade level or subject they teach. Teachers who fail to identify and correct their students' misconceptions may find it extremely difficult to help them understand new material. On the other hand, teachers who anticipate student misconceptions, and who proactively seek them out, can correct these misunderstandings — before they become ingrained in their students' thinking, narrow their views and understanding, and hamper further learning.

Teachers also need to consider any special needs a student may have (such as remediation, acceleration, or second language learning) so that they can design instruction and assessment strategies that will support these needs, help these students recognize and develop confidence in their own abilities, and, as a result, promote optimal learning growth for each individual student.

STUDENTS' INTERESTS AND CULTURAL HERITAGE

How students see the world, participate in learning activities, and absorb new information is, to a great extent, a result of their cultural, social, and familial backgrounds, as well as personal interests and aspirations. Understanding this, and learning as much as possible about these influences, provides teachers with a wealth of information that can be used to bring relevancy to lessons. This understanding also provides clues about what types of teaching strategies are more likely to help students and, conversely, which may be prone to failure.

Teachers who value cultural diversity in the classroom also recognize its usefulness in engaging students. Each student has a unique view of the world, which has been influenced by their cultural background and personal interests. Accomplished teachers understand that they can incorporate this rich diversity into the instructional experiences students share with each other.

At the same time, understanding and responding to cultural differences in sensitive and positive ways can also encourage a sense of mutual respect and trust between teachers and their students, help students feel safe and valued as individuals and, as a result, more ready to risk challenging themselves in the classroom. Long term, your careful treatment of student interests and cultural heritage may also promote tolerance, social responsibility, peaceful conflict resolution, and prepare students for citizenry in a diverse world.

Students bring a variety of talents, needs, expectations, and values with them to the classroom. It's up to you, as their teacher, to learn as much as you can about those diverse and complex aspects of their personalities and skills that will influence their ability and eagerness to learn. You can begin this process by thoroughly understanding these four elements (characteristics of age group, varied approaches to learning, students' skills and knowledge, and students' interests and cultural heritage), and thinking about how they can be applied when you plan and implement instruction and assessments that motivate and encourage students to become active, involved learners who achieve important and lasting learning goals.

HOW STUDENT MOTIVATION AND ENGAGEMENT INFLUENCE LEARNING

Students learn best when they are both motivated to learn and fully engaged in the learning process. In fact, learning experts tell us that, above all else, engagement is an essential prerequisite for developing understanding, particularly when that understanding requires self-discipline, concentration, or complex thinking.[2] So it's important that you understand (1) the role motivation and engagement play in learning; (2) your role as a teacher in developing, encouraging, supporting, and maintaining motivation and engagement in your students; and (3) how becoming skilled at developing a well-informed knowledge of your students can help you accomplish this rather formidable—but essential—responsibility.

You may find it helpful to think about what we mean when we're talking about student motivation and engagement as they relate to successful learning.

Student motivation refers to a student's desire to learn, his or her willingness to participate in the learning process, and the reasons that underlie the student's involvement (or lack of involvement) in learning. These reasons, or motives, may be based on internal motivations, external motivations, or a combination of both.

Motivation affects the amount of time and effort students are willing to devote to learning and mastery. Highly motivated students are willing, even compelled, to learn. They eagerly confront tasks that challenge their abilities and competencies, and they exert intense effort and concentration toward mastering the subject matter at hand—both in school and in life. They enthusiastically embrace learning, and they take on and enjoy new, sometimes difficult, learning

[2] See Tomlinson; also www.ils.northwestern.edu/e-for-e/nodes/NODE-343-pg.html and "Motivating Students to Learn" [electronic version], February 2002, *Infobrief*, 28 [retrieved from http://www.ascd.org/frameinfobrief.html].

opportunities that may require them to make intellectual leaps into unknown territory. (At the very least, they are not overly intimidated by such challenges.) These are the students who always have their homework done on time, volunteer to share their solutions with the entire class, are happy to participate or often initiate class discussions, and connect what they are doing in your class to what they are doing in other classes. They are the same students who bring in newspaper articles or books related to the topic of study (without being asked), present alternative solutions or designs, and independently research and share additional information.

In other words, students who are highly motivated learners are ready to be fully engaged in the learning process. They thirst for knowledge and mastery, have an innate sense of curiosity, and are driven by a natural desire to understand the world around them. They take pride not simply in earning good grades or gaining their teacher's—or their parents'—approval, but in fully understanding the material.[3] They engage in learning for the pure enjoyment of learning in and of itself, and they work hard at it. In short, they are *intrinsically* motivated to learn and master the challenging work before them.

A student who is *extrinsically* motivated, on the other hand, engages in learning out of a need to attain a reward or avoid punishment.[4] Although even a little learning is preferable to no learning, there is compelling evidence that students who are more intrinsically motivated are more likely than extrinsically motivated students to be successful learners. (In fact, some studies have found that extrinsic motivation can actually be *demotivating* and reduce intrinsic motivation.[5]) For example, compared to extrinsically motivated learners, intrinsically motivated learners are more likely to process information at a deeper level, to use logical information-gathering and decision-making strategies, and to prefer moderately challenging tasks.[6] Conversely, students who are motivated to complete a task only to obtain a reward (such as a good grade) or to avoid negative consequences (such as the risk of failure) typically do not work as hard as their intrinsically motivated peers. Moreover, they are unlikely to become engaged learners. As a result, they tend to be more easily frustrated by complex and challenging material, and they are less apt to persevere when facing difficult learning tasks.[7] These students are also at higher risk of dropping out of education, both figuratively and literally.

---

[3] See, for example, Mark Lepper, 1988, "Motivational considerations in the study of instruction. *Cognition and Instruction* (5)4. pp. 289-309.
[4] Lepper, 1988.
[5] See *Problems with Extrinsic Motivation*, http://seamonkey.ed.asu.edu/~jimbo/RIBARY_Folder/problems.htm; see also *Failure of Extrinsic Motivation*, http://www.ils.nwu.edu/e-for-e/nodes/NODE-148-pg.html and *The Impact of Extrinsic Motivation*, http://www.oncourseworkshop.com/Motivation004.htm
[6] Linda S. Lumsden, Student motivation to learn. ERIC Digest, Number 92.
[7] See www.nwrel.org

In general, how motivated are the students with whom you work? Record at least two examples that support your conclusion.

> *Research has shown that motivated students, students who are engaged in the learning process, tend to demonstrate understanding of information at a deeper, more complex level and tend to retain information and concepts longer.*

Research has shown that motivated students, students who are engaged in the learning process, tend to demonstrate understanding of information at a deeper, more complex level and tend to retain information and concepts longer. These students are more likely to take on tasks that challenge their knowledge and abilities, to direct their own learning, to seek and develop solutions to complex problems, and to show greater creativity and cognitive flexibility. They are also more likely to be satisfied with their school experiences, to complete their education, and to seek out new learning opportunities, even after completing school.[8]

Given this strong link between motivation and achievement, it is clearly imperative that teachers develop a strong sense of their role in facilitating and fostering student motivation and engagement in learning. And make no mistake about it: The part you play is critical. Whatever you do, whatever happens in the classroom, will transform—for better or worse—the level of motivation and engagement your students bring with them as they approach each new learning experience.

FACTORS THAT INFLUENCE STUDENT ENGAGEMENT AND MOTIVATION

Engaging and motivating students begins with understanding *what* will engage and motivate them—which strategies, practices, or approaches are likely to trigger their curiosity and desire to learn, and which are likely to "turn them off." Researchers and educators alike have found, through classroom experience as well as investigation, that the activities most likely to capture students' attention, the ones they are most likely to work hard at (even when they find the concepts

---

[8] See Heather Voke, "Motivating Students to Learn" [electronic version], February 2002 *Infobrief*, 28 [Retrieved from http://www.ascd.org/frameinfobrief.html]. See also *Increasing Student Engagement and Motivation: From Time-on-Task to Homework*, www.nwrel.org/rquestions/oct00./intro.html and *Education Reforms and Students at Risk: A Review of the Current State of the Art - January 1994*, http://www.ed.gov/pubs/EdReformStudies/EdReforms/chap5b.html

difficult) and to retain, are the ones they find fun, interesting, personally meaningful, and relevant in some way. They are the activities that students find challenging but attainable, that relate to their own personal goals and aspirations, and that accommodate their individual learning preferences.

Clearly, these are the kinds of learning activities you will want to develop for your own class. But to do this successfully, you must first take time to develop a substantive working knowledge of your students, both individually and as a group. Only through understanding your students' backgrounds, interests, goals, ambitions, personalities, and approaches to learning can you begin to determine which approaches will work best to engage and motivate your students, and which may result in frustration, boredom, and—at the worst—disengagement.

Education experts agree that many factors affect students' motivation to work and learn; some of these are driven by external factors while others are a function of each student's own internal processes. They include the students' home environments and family attitudes toward learning, their school-related successes and failures, and the sources to which the students attribute those successes (their own effort and hard work versus good luck) or failures (such as their own lack of ability, bad luck, or not trying hard enough). Schoolwide and classroom goals, policies, procedures, and climate also play a critical role in how students feel about school and schoolwork, as do teachers' attitudes, expectations, beliefs about learning, and instructional approaches.

Students' own developmental stages, personal learning styles, and levels of self-confidence and self-esteem, as well as their individual personalities (such as their innate tendency to be patient, persistent, and willing to take risks, or to be easily frustrated and quickly bored, for example) have a strong influence on their attitudes about school and learning. Their interest in the subject matter and their perception of its usefulness and relevance in their own lives also influence how engaged they are in the learning process. Although you have little control over many of the conditions and experiences that affect your students' attitudes toward learning, there are some critical areas in which you, as their teacher, can inspire your students' willingness to think, work, learn, and grow—despite any obstacles they may be facing. Your ability to choose and use teaching strategies that support

Your ability to choose and use teaching strategies that support your students' individual approaches to learning, to connect lessons to your students' interests and real-life experiences, to present material in a way that is challenging yet attainable for them, and to convince your students that they are capable of achieving success will have a profound effect on their ability and willingness to learn.

your students' individual approaches to learning, to connect lessons to your students' interests and real-life experiences, to present material in a way that is challenging yet attainable for them, and to convince your students that they are capable of achieving success will have a profound effect on their ability and willingness to learn. But to do this, you need to "know your students."

An Invitation to Reflect

Describe the general level of self-confidence you see in the group(s) of students you teach. What do you see as evidence of that self-confidence level?

How Knowledge of Students Can Help You Engage and Motivate Your Students

Students, whatever their age or level of academic fitness, are puzzling, complex, often contradictory individuals. They are individuals, with individual needs. And they grow and change intellectually, socially, and emotionally, as well as physically, from day to day, year to year—even from one classroom to the next. Some exhibit an unquenchable thirst for knowledge while others—although clearly capable—either coast along, applying just enough effort to get by or, worse, tune out of the learning process completely. Still others will start out as enthusiastic, eager learners but gradually become apathetic and detached. Some have obvious learning challenges and, for many reasons, struggle to keep up with their peers despite their best efforts. And, of course, there are those students who seem to excel no matter what the circumstance.

Your classroom, if it's like most, is made up of a mixture of all of these personalities and situations. But, no matter what challenges or gifts your students bring with them to the classroom, they each deserve a chance to learn, to develop, and to challenge their abilities, and to succeed. Indeed, they deserve to have the opportunity to exceed expectation and to excel.

Whether excelling in all subjects or struggling to understand basic concepts, every student has the capacity to grow and engage in learning. Every student has a unique set of gifts waiting to be nurtured and cultivated. Your challenge is to find and use the most effective mixture of tools for supporting and encouraging your students, both individually and as a class, so that they can become (or remain) engaged, motivated learners. In so doing, you will give them the best possible chance to develop their own innate talents, skills, and passions—and, most of all, to learn.

This means finding ways to keep your students interested in both the lesson at hand and learning in general. It also means finding ways to work with and develop your students' natural ways of dealing with information, problems, and the world around them. And, because the learning needs of each student are unique and ever-changing, you must become adept at choosing and using multiple approaches to teaching.

Your challenge is to find and use the most effective mixture of tools for supporting and encouraging your students, both individually and as a class, so that they can become (or remain) engaged, motivated learners.

It's all well and good to have a broad repertoire of teaching strategies designed to address an assortment of learning requirements. But to be most effective, those strategies must be thoughtfully chosen with specific purposes and situations in mind, including the learning needs of individual students, as well as of the class as a whole. For example, a teacher might introduce a new unit of study by first asking students to brainstorm[9], in pairs or small groups, what they already know about this topic. Once the brainstorming session has reached a satisfactory conclusion, a whole-class sharing would follow, with the teacher recording students' prior knowledge (or misconceptions) on a wall chart.

In other words, in addition to considering the lesson and subject matter being covered, you need to think about your students. What do they already know about the subject—or think that they know? What will they find interesting? Conversely, what will they find downright tedious? How can you make every lesson exciting, relevant, and approachable for your students while still advancing important learning goals? What instructional strategies will help a student who is having particular difficulty with the concepts being covered?

To answer these questions you need to start with the students themselves. You need to find out, to the extent possible:

- where your students are in terms of their intellectual, social, and emotional development, and whether they have any special learning needs

- how they feel most comfortable learning (for example: in a quiet atmosphere or with music playing, in a brightly lit room or with soft illumination, alone or in a small group of peers, sitting at a desk or moving around, through reading, listening, or hands-on)

---

[9] Brainstorming is a group process in which everybody's ideas are accepted (without judgment) and recorded. Debate and discussion should not be part of a brainstorming session. For more information, check out http://www.demon.co.uk/mindtool/brainstm.html, http://members.ozemail.com.au/~caveman/Creative/Techniques/brainstorm.htm, and http://edweb.sdsu.edu/people/bdodge/scaffold/BS/Brainstorming.html#Brainstorming.

- what they know and what they don't know, what they can do and what they can't do, and whether they have developed any misconceptions or misunderstandings that could stand in the way of learning

- what they are interested in or passionate about, both in school and outside of school

- what their cultural backgrounds are and how these backgrounds may affect how they feel about learning as well as how they see the world, participate in learning activities, or absorb new information

- how any issues or events taking place in your students lives are affecting their attitudes about learning

AN INVITATION TO REFLECT

What misconceptions are typical of the age group of the students you teach? What misconceptions are typical of the subject matter you teach?

WHY DO I NEED THIS INFORMATION?

Your students need and expect you to present information in a way that is understandable and relevant to them. That's not as easy as it may first seem. Today's classrooms, as you well know, serve students with every imaginable background, skill level, ability, need, interest, personality, and ambition. These students present their teachers with a vast array of unique and multifaceted personal characteristics that can all-too-easily thrive or whither under specific learning conditions — learning conditions that may affect their peers in a completely different manner. And it's up to you, their teacher, to find a way to help each of these students — no matter how different one may be from another — achieve his or her fullest potential as a learner.

> *Your students need and expect you to present information in a way that is understandable and relevant to them.*

Easy? Absolutely not. But, by developing a sound understanding of the elements that affect how and what students learn, as well as a more complete knowledge of what each of your students knows and can do, you are laying the groundwork for being able to plan curriculum, instructional strategies, and assessments that are appropriate, challenging (but not overwhelming), interesting, stimulating, and relevant. This student-focused instructional approach will help you motivate and guide your students to grow as learners, so that they can achieve—or exceed—their own learning goals and expectations and, ultimately, take ownership of their own learning.

> This student-focused instructional approach will help you motivate and guide your students to grow as learners, so that they can achieve—or exceed—their own learning goals and expectations and, ultimately, take ownership of their own learning.

Specifically, knowledge of your students helps you:

- assess student strengths and learning areas on which to focus
- identify and address student difficulties (academic, social, behavioral, emotional, and physical)
- determine student readiness to learn new content
- engage students in relevant, authentic learning
- motivate students to achieve higher learning goals

TODAY'S DIVERSE CLASSROOM

Today's classroom is a dramatically different place than it was 50 years ago. The students who come through the classroom door encompass a far broader range of cultural and socioeconomic backgrounds, family situations and support systems, physical and intellectual abilities, experiences, and expectations. Teachers must address a greater variety of student needs than ever before. Many of today's students lack the experiences and support mechanisms teachers once took for granted. At the same time, they have been exposed to a far greater array of experiences and information—for better or for worse—than yesterday's teachers could ever have imagined.

In a word, today's students are diverse—in every aspect encompassed by the word. Every one of these students deserves and is entitled to the best education teachers can provide. Recognizing, honoring, and accommodating each student's individual learning needs is the only way to provide each and every student equal access to education. Having a more complete and informed understanding of who their students are, where they come from, and where they hope to go is a small but vital part of educators ensuring that all students have an equal shot at educational excellence.

Just as it is imperative that you understand your students' backgrounds, it is useful to you, too, to know from what point, from what level of skill, you are beginning this course of study. The minicourse provides you with a level-of-performance scale to consider.

A Level-of-Performance Scale

For each of the 22 components described in *Enhancing Professional Practice: A Framework for Teaching*, there is an accompanying level-of-performance scale. The level-of-performance scale associated with the component "Demonstrating Knowledge of Students" appears as Figure 1.1 of this workbook. The four levels of the scale—**unsatisfactory**, **basic**, **proficient**, and **distinguished**—are not intended to represent equidistant points on a continuum, nor do they represent developmental stages. Instead, they are written to describe four typical levels of performance as teachers gain experience and acquire skill in their craft. One teacher's practice for any of the components could fall over several levels. When conducting a self-assessment of your own teaching practice, it is important to think in terms of your *current* practice, as well as what is *typical* of your day-to-day teaching experience.

The **unsatisfactory** level is used to describe a performance that demonstrates little or no knowledge of students' age-group expectations, backgrounds, skills, or interests, nor knowledge of why that information would be valuable to instruction and student learning.

The **basic** performance level indicates a partial knowledge of students' age-group expectations, backgrounds, skills, and interests, and an attempt to use that knowledge in planning instruction for the class as a whole.

The **proficient** level represents a solid, thorough knowledge of students' age-group expectations, backgrounds, skills, and interests, and clear evidence of its application to instructional and assessment strategies for groups of students.

The **distinguished** level describes thorough knowledge of students' age-group expectations, backgrounds, skills, and interests, and the ability to apply that knowledge when planning for individual student learning and assessment.

The four levels of performance outlined in this scale, and the skills described at each level, can be useful in professional dialogue about teaching, as well as for identifying individual areas in need of work and focus. The descriptions of teaching at each performance level can be used to stimulate powerful and relevant discussions about effective teaching practice among professionals.

Level-of-performance scales let you momentarily isolate an aspect of teaching practice so that you can reflect upon it and assess your strengths as well as your needs for advancement. However, teachers who achieve a proficient level of skill in any given domain understand that, during daily practice, all components are interdependent and interwoven.

| ELEMENT | LEVEL OF PERFORMANCE | | | |
	UNSATISFACTORY	BASIC	PROFICIENT	DISTINGUISHED
KNOWLEDGE OF CHARACTERISTICS OF AGE GROUP	Teacher displays minimal knowledge of developmental characteristics of age group.	Teacher displays generally accurate knowledge of developmental characteristics of age group.	Teacher displays thorough understanding of typical developmental characteristics of age group as well as exceptions to general patterns.	Teacher displays knowledge of typical developmental characteristics of age group, exceptions to the patterns, and the extent to which each student follows patterns.
KNOWLEDGE OF STUDENTS' VARIED APPROACHES TO LEARNING	Teacher is unfamiliar with the different approaches to learning that students exhibit.	Teacher displays general understanding of the different approaches to learning that students exhibit.	Teacher displays solid understanding of the different approaches to learning that different students exhibit.	Teacher uses, where appropriate, knowledge of students' varied approaches to learning in instructional planning.
KNOWLEDGE OF STUDENTS' SKILLS AND KNOWLEDGE	Teacher displays little knowledge of students' skills and knowledge and does not indicate that such knowledge is valuable.	Teacher recognizes the value of understanding students' skills and knowledge but displays this knowledge for the class only as a whole.	Teacher displays knowledge of students' skills and knowledge for groups of students and recognizes the value of this knowledge.	Teacher displays knowledge of students' skills and knowledge for each student, including those with special needs.
KNOWLEDGE OF STUDENTS' INTERESTS AND CULTURAL HERITAGE	Teacher displays little knowledge of students' interests and cultural heritage and does not indicate that such knowledge is valuable.	Teacher recognizes the value of understanding students' interests and cultural heritage but displays this knowledge for the class only as a whole.	Teacher displays knowledge of the interests and cultural heritage of groups of students and recognizes the value of this knowledge.	Teacher displays knowledge of the interests and cultural heritage of each student.

Figure 1.1: A Level-of-Performance Scale for Demonstrating Knowledge of Students (from *Enhancing Professional Practice: A Framework for Teaching* by Charlotte Danielson).

This level-of-performance scale will help you identify and think about the ways in which you know your students, and your ability to use that information to plan effective instruction and assessment. Like most teachers, you will probably be stronger in some areas than others. The Related Activities that follow ask you to evaluate your current practice and then set some goals for gaining further knowledge about the two students you will select for focus later during this minicourse. The work you complete for the minicourse will guide you in deepening your knowledge of these students and then applying your learning to better your understanding of all of your students and their individual learning needs.

Directions: The following activities are intended to help you identify areas for growth in understanding the importance of knowing your students. The activities should be completed sequentially and in a manner conducive with your personal learning style.

COMPLETED

1.1 Using **My Minicourse Journal**, which follows, reflect on and assess your current teaching practice as it relates to "Demonstrating Knowledge of Students." If you teach more than one group of students, select one class period for your assessment. Think of your class as a whole as you evaluate your knowledge of your students.

1.2 From the class you selected to use for your self-assessment, identify two students who you would like to understand more thoroughly so that they will be more likely to succeed during this school year. You may want to select a student because of problematic behavior (e.g., lack of achievement, disruptive classroom behavior, and/or weak or inconsistent work habits) or because you believe you need more or better knowledge about the student in order to connect with him or her. You may want to help a student grow as a learner, or as a more confident member of a peer group. Explain your reasons for selecting each of these students using the **Selection of Students for Focus** chart that follows.

		COMPLETED
1.3	Determine your current knowledge of each of these students for each element by noting specific information you already have and how that information has impacted your current practice. For example, you may have tailored assignments to the readiness level or interests of these students. Use the first two columns of the chart entitled **Knowledge of Students** to record this information. Use the third column, "Additional Information," to identify additional information that would be helpful to collect for each of the four elements as they relate to these two students.	
1.4	Review one or more articles about any of the four types of knowledge about students to better understand the students selected for focus. The resource list provided in Appendix B can help you locate articles for this activity. Alternatively, you may find articles online, in a professional journal, or elsewhere. Use the **What I Learned From Other Resources** chart to record learning.	
1.5	If you wish, discuss this topic with other teachers. To help you recall what was said, take notes during the discussion using the **What I Learned from Other Resources** chart.	

my minicourse
Journal

1. Select a class or group of students with whom you work. Identify the class or group in the space below.

2. Refer to the level-of-performance scale provided in Part I (Figure 1.1). For each of the four elements listed below, how would you rate your current proficiency for demonstrating knowledge of students?

Element	Level-of-Performance Rating
Knowledge of Characteristics of Age Group	_____
Knowledge of Students' Varied Approaches to Learning	_____
Knowledge of Students' Skills and Knowledge	_____
Knowledge of Students' Interests and Cultural Heritage	_____

3. List the strengths that your self-assessment has revealed and next to each, provide at least one example.

4. Which element in this component are you most comfortable with?

5. Which element are you least comfortable with? Why?

6. List the areas in which you would like to improve.

7. In one to three sentences, summarize the manner in which you currently demonstrate knowledge of your students.

8. *How does your cultural background influence the way you see the world and participate in learning activities?*

9. *Recall a time when your background knowledge either positively or negatively affected a learning experience that you were involved in (such as a graduate class, professional seminar, or an adult workshop).*

10. *How do your own interests and talents influence what and how you learn?*

11. *What is the relationship between knowledge of students and designing instruction around content standards?*

Student A: _____

Reasons for selection:

Student B: _____

Reasons for selection:

Student A: _____

How long have you been working with Student A?

In what class (subject area) do you teach Student A?

ELEMENT	CURRENT INFORMATION	IMPACT ON CURRENT INSTRUCTION	ADDITIONAL INFORMATION
KNOWLEDGE OF CHARACTERISTICS OF AGE GROUP			
KNOWLEDGE OF STUDENTS' VARIED APPROACHES TO LEARNING			
KNOWLEDGE OF STUDENTS' SKILLS AND KNOWLEDGE			
KNOWLEDGE OF STUDENTS' INTERESTS AND CULTURAL HERITAGE			

To what extent is Student A motivated to learn? What tells you so?

Is there anything else you would like to note about Student A?

Student B: _____

How long have you been working with Student B?

In what class (subject area) do you teach Student B?

ELEMENT	CURRENT INFORMATION	IMPACT ON CURRENT INSTRUCTION	ADDITIONAL INFORMATION
KNOWLEDGE OF CHARACTERISTICS OF AGE GROUP			
KNOWLEDGE OF STUDENTS' VARIED APPROACHES TO LEARNING			
KNOWLEDGE OF STUDENTS' SKILLS AND KNOWLEDGE			
KNOWLEDGE OF STUDENTS' INTERESTS AND CULTURAL HERITAGE			

To what extent is Student B motivated to learn? What tells you so?

Is there anything else you would like to note about Student B?

WHAT I LEARNED FROM OTHER RESOURCES	
RESOURCE	INPUT

PART II

OBJECTIVES:

- UNDERSTAND HOW THE FOUR ELEMENTS THAT COMPRISE THE "DEMONSTRATING KNOWLEDGE OF STUDENTS" FRAMEWORK COMPONENT SUPPORT A STUDENT-FOCUSED APPROACH TO INSTRUCTION.

- UNDERSTAND HOW A STUDENT-FOCUSED APPROACH TO INSTRUCTION CAN IMPROVE LEARNING.

- EXAMINE THE VARIOUS TOOLS TEACHERS CAN USE TO BROADEN THEIR KNOWLEDGE OF THEIR STUDENTS.

- UNDERSTAND THE "DEMONSTRATING KNOWLEDGE OF STUDENTS" INVESTIGATIVE PROCESS.

DEVELOPING YOUR KNOWLEDGE BASE

Making information interesting, relevant, and challenging (but not too challenging), and presenting it in such a way that your students can connect with it, is key to engaging students in the learning process. But students are individuals and, as such, very different from one another — fundamentally different in how they learn and what they find interesting, meaningful, and worth putting effort into.

What does this mean? It means that successful teaching — teaching that gives each student a chance to learn, a chance to grow, and a chance to succeed — requires more than knowing the material you're teaching or having a diverse repertoire of teaching strategies, approaches, and tools. While these are essential aspects of good teaching, they are ineffective without knowing your students' interests, their aspirations, and how they feel about learning and why. Also, before you can determine which strategies are appropriate or which tools will be most effective, you need to know where your students are in terms of what they know and don't know as it relates to the content they are learning.

Once you have this information, you can use it to inform and guide your lesson plans and activities, and assessment methods. As you become more experienced and comfortable using the knowledge you have of your students, you will find that you can use it to help students connect new learning to what they already know or to their interests outside of school, such as hobbies that are of personal interest. This information will also help you gain an understanding of what learning strategies are most likely to work best for your students. Most of all, you can use your knowledge of your students to respond quickly and effectively to both planned and spontaneous learning opportunities and situations. For example, a language arts teacher knows that a specific class of eighth-grade students has a passion for art, drama, or music. As a culminating project for a unit on poetry reading, the teacher taps into this passion by giving the students the opportunity to show what they've learned about poetry through any one of a variety of expressions. For example, some students might create their own poem, others might illustrate a poem or give an oral presentation explaining their interpretation of the poem. Still others might present a creative dance or musical interpretation of the poem.

AN INVITATION TO REFLECT

Recall a recent spontaneous learning opportunity in your classroom. How might you have used your knowledge of your students' interests to make your response in that situation more interesting and engaging for your students?

Of course, as you probably know all too well, gathering this sort of information isn't as easy as it sounds. Although younger students (those in kindergarten and the earlier years of elementary school) may be eager to talk about the things that excite them, older students typically aren't as willing to share this information with their teachers. Even trickier is gaining an accurate picture of, for example, students' levels of social or emotional development or what approaches to learning work best for them. When was the last time a student told you, "Hey, I need to tell you that I'm basically too insecure with where I fit in with my peers to feel comfortable leading a group" or "Look, the reason I'm fidgeting over here is because I don't learn well linguistically. I'm more of a 'bodily-kinesthetic' kind of kid"? More likely, what you knew (or thought you knew) about these students was based on subtle behavioral signals you had observed in the classroom or elsewhere. But wouldn't you feel better if you had concrete, valid evidence of how your students are likely to respond in specific learning environments, of what techniques are more likely to engage them, of how they relate to the world around them?

Think back on one or two occasions in the classroom in which a student was having difficulty grasping a concept or was clearly disengaged. Try to recall any signals the student may have been sending that told you this lesson wasn't working for this student. How did you react?

Gathering this kind of information—information that will help you facilitate active, engaged learning—requires a thoughtfully planned-out approach. This is an investigation, of sorts, into who your students are, where they are, what they know, what they don't know, and how and in what venue they learn best. As is the case with any good investigation, those conducting it need to have a clear understanding of the many "investigative" tools at their disposal. They must know how to use those tools effectively, the kind of information those tools can elicit, and their limitations. Equally as important is knowing how to interpret the information these tools provide and, eventually, how to purposefully and effectively apply that information to, in this case, instruction, curriculum, and assessment.

Finally, because students are complex and ever-changing individuals, and because learning is an ongoing, dynamic process, it will rarely, if ever, be enough to conduct a single investigation using one individual tool. Developing an accurate and therefore multidimensional knowledge of your students will require ongoing investigation using a variety of investigative tools.

> Developing an accurate and therefore multidimensional knowledge of your students will require ongoing investigation using a variety of investigative tools.

However, it takes time to develop an informed understanding of these tools and confidence in using them. Unless you are familiar with many of the tools we will be discussing in this minicourse, it is best to begin by focusing on learning about one or two tools, and using those tools in your practice. On the other hand, if you currently use many of these tools and confidently apply them to your practice, you may find that this minicourse offers you an opportunity to refine your current skills or to focus on new areas.

THE TOOLS OF YOUR INVESTIGATION

Gaining knowledge of the many aspects of your students is an essential step in developing an engaging, student-focused learning environment. You may already gather information subconsciously about your students. But it's much more effective and efficient to gather this information in a purposeful, methodical, structured manner, and to keep a record of that information so that you can refer to it on a regular basis as well as when one or more of your students are having difficulty.

Teachers have a host of "investigative" tools that they can use for developing useful, learning-relevant knowledge of their students. As is the case with tools, they each have their individual purposes and each yield specific products; in this case, particular kinds of information about students.

Although some of these tools are easier to understand and use than others, they all require study, understanding, and practice in order to use them most effectively.

This minicourse is designed to give you insight into various tools. However, some of the tools that will be covered require extensive study beyond the parameters of this course to be fully understood and applied. In such cases, this minicourse will introduce you to the basic concepts of these tools and then direct you toward useful resources that you can use for further, deeper study.

The investigative tools discussed in this section fall into two categories:

Organizational Models

These include models, taxonomies, and theories that attempt to explain how people perceive, think, and gain understanding of the world around them. They include:

- Developmental models
- Learning-style models

Investigative Methods

These are specific "tools of the trade"—methods you can use to gather information about your students. They include:

■ "Kidwatching"

■ Records

■ People and other resources (colleagues, family members, other professionals)

ORGANIZATIONAL MODELS

DEVELOPMENTAL MODELS

Every student is unique, with an individual temperament, learning style, cultural background, range of interests, and set of life experiences. But even though these differences can be profound, children are also surprisingly similar to one another in many ways. Among other things, how students develop and grow physically and how they build capacity to assimilate and process information tend to follow a relatively universal and predictable sequence. Developmental models attempt to explain how people (for our purposes, students) perceive, think, and gain understanding of the world around them. Once you've taken the time to understand these models on more than a surface level, you will find that they can help you develop your knowledge of your students' age-group characteristics. They can also offer plenty of insight into your students' varied approaches to learning, and how to support those approaches.

Among other things, how students develop and grow physically and how they build capacity to assimilate and process information tend to follow a relatively universal and predictable sequence.

These models are typically complex, and they should be studied over time and within the context of other developmental theories. Although a full discussion of developmental models and their implications is beyond the scope of this minicourse, this section of the minicourse introduces you to some of the more well-known models and offers a brief discussion of their main concepts. Additional resources that you can use for further study are listed in Appendix B.

Even though these concepts are complex, they are well worth considering and spending extra time to understand more completely. Among other things, they can provide insight into the range of cognitive, social, and verbal abilities that can be expected within an age group, as well as what kinds of behaviors and cognitive processes are typical of most children at a given age. When equipped with this information, teachers are better able to plan lessons that are age-appropriate and developmentally appropriate for their students. These models can also help teachers understand the significance of certain student behaviors and responses. For example, middle-school teachers know the importance of peer relationships to this age group and plan group activities that factor in this developmental model.

These models can also help you recognize when students aren't moving along as one might anticipate, and give you an opportunity to respond by adapting your lessons or strategies accordingly. For example, after further investigation you may learn that a student who has been struggling with open-ended test questions is actually having trouble with the physical act of gripping a pencil and the physical act of writing. An occupational therapist is able to help the student adjust his grip so that he can write legibly without as much effort and frustration. While he is learning this new skill, you allow him to dictate some of his answers to the test questions.

It is critical, however, that you don't overemphasize the expectations postulated by these models.

It is critical, however, that you don't overemphasize the expectations postulated by these models. Although it is helpful to know the general sequences of development these theories present, it is even more important to look at your students as individuals, and to use these models to get a general sense of how your students fit in each of the developmental continua so that you can plan your instruction accordingly.

PIAGET'S THEORY OF CHILDHOOD COGNITIVE DEVELOPMENT

The most widely known and perhaps most influential developmental theory is Jean Piaget's theory of childhood cognitive development. Piaget proposed that there is a progressive developmental sequence to how a child thinks. This sequence, he argued, consists of four age-related stages. Each of these stages has distinctive characteristics that permit specific ways of thinking. The differences between these stages are *qualitative*—that is, at each successive stage, a child doesn't learn to do things better, but to do different things altogether. Further, according to this theory, a child's cognitive performance depends more on which stage of development the child has entered than on the specific task being performed.

Piaget also argued that, in order for learning to occur, an individual must assimilate new information into existing cognitive structures. That is to say, there must be overlap between a new experience and prior knowledge. This concept has implications for engaging and facilitating learning, particularly in terms of helping students connect new information with what they already know.

PIAGET'S STAGES OF CHILDHOOD COGNITIVE DEVELOPMENT		
APPROXIMATE AGE	STAGE	MAJOR CHARACTERISTICS
Birth–2 years	Sensorimotor	• Builds an understanding (concepts) about the world and how it works through physical interaction with the environment. • Does not know physical objects remain in existence even when out of sight (object permanence)—for example, if a ball is covered by a blanket, the child does not know it still exists.
2–7 years	Preoperational	• Represents things with words and images, but cannot reason with logic. • Lacks the concept of conservation. For example, suppose a child is presented with two rows of four objects, but one row is lengthened by spreading the objects apart. If asked which row has more, the child will likely point to the longer row, because children in this stage cannot simultaneously focus on both number and length. • Exhibits egocentric thought and language.
7–12 years	Concrete Operational	• Can think logically about concrete events. • Gains abilities to solve conservation and reversibility tasks (e.g., 3+2= 5 and 5-2=3).
12 years and older	Formal Operational	• Develops ability to think abstractly and to consider many possibilities for a given condition, hence can solve complex and hypothetical problems involving abstract operations. Can recognize and identify a problem. • Can plan and think ahead. • Early in this stage, there is a return to egocentric thought.

Figure 2.1: Piaget's Stages of Childhood Cognitive Development

Recent studies have begun to cast some doubt on whether children actually go through the stages in the way Piaget postulated. Developmental psychologists now believe that performance varies greatly within each stage and depends more on a child's acquisition and development of language, real-world knowledge, perception, and decision rules. In addition, theorists now believe that not every individual reaches the formal operational stage of development.[10] Still, Piaget's work continues to have a profound impact on instruction. Many pre-school and primary programs are modeled on his theory, which has influenced the constructivist approach to learning as well as discovery learning approaches.

---

[10] Piaget's Stage Theory of Development, http://web.psych.ualberta.ca/%7Emike/Pearl_Street/Dictionary/contents/P/piaget's_stages.html

How does your experience with students compare with Piaget's theory?

DISCOVERY LEARNING

> *In discovery learning, learning takes place when students are not presented the subject matter in its final form, but allowed to develop, discover and organize it themselves.*

Discovery learning is an inquiry-based approach to instruction through which students interact with their environment by exploring and manipulating objects, wrestling with questions, or performing experiments. In discovery learning, learning takes place when students are not presented the subject matter in its final form, but allowed to develop, discover and organize it themselves. This occurs most notably in problem-solving situations, where the learner draws on his or her own experiences and prior knowledge to discover new information or skills. This approach to learning encourages students to ask questions and formulate their own tentative answers, and to deduce general principles from practical examples or experience. Over the years, teachers have found that it is most successful when students have prerequisite knowledge and undergo structured experiences.[11]

In a typical discovery learning science lesson, for example, the teacher plans a science experiment in which the students must make their own hypotheses. They perform the experiment while gathering data, all while learning new concepts and drawing conclusions. The teacher provides guidance, but no answers.

Jerome Bruner (1962) wrote that "emphasis on discovery in learning has precisely the effect on the learner of leading him to be a constructionist, to organize what he is encountering in a manner not only designed to discover regularity and relatedness, but also to avoid the kind of information drift that fails to keep account of the uses to which information might have to be put." Dewey and Piaget, among others, also support this approach to teaching and learning.

---

[11] See www.nwlink.com/~donclark/hrd/history/discovery.htm and www.discovery.utexas.edu/dlp

CONSTRUCTIVISM

Constructivism is a philosophy of learning founded on the premise that knowledge and understanding is constructed within the mind of the learner. Constructivists believe that people generate their own set of "rules" and "mental models," which they use to make sense of their experiences. In other words, learning is simply the process of adjusting one's mental models to accommodate new experiences. Constructivists further believe that people learn best by actively constructing their own understanding, based on their own prior knowledge and experiences and understandings. A constructivist classroom, then, encourages students to be actively involved in the learning process, and they are given opportunities to build their own knowledge based on their own prior knowledge, understandings, and background. Further, constructivists argue that in order to teach well, teachers must understand the mental models that students use to perceive the world and the assumptions they make to support those models.[12] This contrasts with an approach that treats students as passive learners who *receive* knowledge. For more information on constructivism, check out the suggested reading in Appendix B.

> *A constructivist classroom, then, encourages students to be actively involved in the learning process, and they are given opportunities to build their own knowledge based on their own prior knowledge, understandings, and background.*

AN INVITATION TO REFLECT

How could you use your knowledge of your students to plan a lesson based on the discovery learning approach?

BRUNER'S THEORY OF CHILDREN'S COGNITIVE DEVELOPMENT

Jerome Bruner is one of the leading representatives of the constructivist school of learning. Central to his thinking is the idea that any concept can be taught effectively in some intellectually honest form to children at any age, provided the material is presented in a way that is appropriate for the student (Bruner, 1960).[13] He also argues that learning is an active process in which learners construct new ideas or concepts based on current knowledge. The learner selects and transforms information, constructs hypotheses, and makes decisions, relying on his or her cognitive structure (schema, mental models). It is the learner's cognitive structure that provides meaning and organization to experiences and allows the learner to make mental leaps beyond the information given.

Bruner theorizes that children's intellectual development usually follows a step-by-step progression through three modes of reasoning that correspond to developmental stages: enactive, iconic, and symbolic, in that order. These stages, he contends, are not necessarily age-dependent, nor are they exactly the same for each individual. He believes they are each as dominant during each developmental phase, but present and accessible throughout. According to Bruner, developmental growth involves mastering each of these increasingly more complex modes and becoming skilled in translating between each mode.

- The **enactive** stage is the earliest stage, in which very young children understand best in terms of their own actions. As children learn to role over, sit up, or manipulate objects, they learn to do so through their own actions. While this mode is present in all ages, it is most dominant in the earliest years. This dominance is not limited to children; many adults can learn to perform a variety of motor tasks (typing, sewing a shirt, operating a lawn mower) that they cannot describe in iconic (picture) or symbolic (word) form.

- The **iconic** stage typically develops when the child is around two or three years of age. In this stage, concrete mental images represent objects and events. This may explain why it is often helpful to use diagrams or illustrations to explain new concepts.

- The **symbolic** stage usually develops when a child is about seven years old. Knowledge is stored as words, mathematical symbols, or some other symbol system. Upon reaching this stage, the child has developed the capacity for abstract thought.[14]

[13] Bruner, Jerome. (1960). *The Process of Education. Toward a Theory of Instruction* (1966)...; Jerome Bruner: A Web overview, http://au.geocities.com/vanunoo/Humannature/bruner.html; Counterpoint: Cognitivism, http://www.educ.drake.edu/doc/pedagogy/student_papers/craig_reed/defcog.html
[14] Jerome Bruner, http://www.geocities.com/kaflynn2001/bruner_general.html; Beckman, Marrian, Multiple Ways of Knowing: Howard Gardner's Theory of Multiple Intelligences Extend and Enhance Student Learning, article posted in Earlychildhood.com, http://www.earlychildhood.com/Articles/index.cfm?FuseAction=Article&A=19

Bruner notes that "there is no unique sequence for all learners, and the optimum in any particular case will depend upon a variety of factors, including past learning, stage of development, nature of the material, and individual differences" (1966, p. 49).

Recently, Bruner has expanded his thinking to encompass the social and cultural aspects of learning. He argues that people are social beings and, through social interaction, they acquire a framework for interpreting experiences.

Spiral Curriculum

Application to teaching: In order for a student to effectively learn a given body of knowledge, curriculum must be designed in such a way as to structure the learning from unit to unit, and from year to year. As the student progresses in competency or grade level, the body of knowledge being studied should progress; that is, with each grade level, the curriculum should build upon skills and knowledge learned each year. This is also known as "spiraled curriculum."

Spiral curriculum, as defined by Bruner, refers to a curriculum that revisits the same topics but in greater depth and complexity each time, often at different grade levels or stages of development, depending on the interest and background of the learner.

Lev Vygotsky

The major premise of Lev Vygotsky's Social Cognition Model is that culture is a principal determinant of individual development. People are primarily social beings, who are born into and grow up in a social environment. That social environment (including family environment), along with social interactions, play a fundamental role in cognitive development. For example, symbols vary across cultures and this variance leads to differences in the kinds of mental functions typically developed by individuals within a culture. For example, people from different cultures tend to categorize objects in different ways — one culture may classify plants, for example, according to their use, another according to appearance, and so on. There also tends to be cultural differences in how people think; for example, some cultures tend to think much more linearly than others.[15]

According to Vygotsky, this life-long process of learning is too complex to be defined by stages and entails a process he calls the Zone of Proximal Development. Put simply, this Zone of Proximal Development is the difference between what a learner can do independently and what can be accomplished cognitively with guidance from a more knowledgeable individual, such as a teacher. In essence, the student follows the teacher's example, and gradually

---

[15] Vygotsky and Social Cognition, www.funderstanding.com/vygotsky.cfm; Social Development Theory, http://tip.psychology.org/vygotsky.html

> Put simply, this Zone of Proximal Development is the difference between what a learner can do independently and what can be accomplished cognitively with guidance from a more knowledgeable individual, such as a teacher.

develops the ability to do new tasks without help or assistance. Initially, the person (in this case, the teacher) interacting with the child assumes most of the responsibility for guiding the task, but gradually the child assumes most or all of the responsibility. So, for learning to happen, there must be an opportunity for the student and the teacher to interact or collaborate. Vygotsky believed that what children can do with the assistance of others is even more indicative of their mental development than what they can do alone.[16]

AN INVITATION TO REFLECT

Think about your own daily teaching practice. In what ways do you provide student opportunities to interact or collaborate with you?

DAVID AUSUBEL

David Ausubel was influenced by Piaget's cognitive development theory, and developed his instructional models based on cognitive structures. Ausubel believed that, in order to make learning meaningful, students must relate new information to what they already know. He further argued that it is the job of the teacher to structure learning, select appropriate materials for students, and present learning material in a well-organized manner that integrates new material with existing knowledge.

Ausubel's "advanced organizer" approach to teaching is a cognitive strategy for promoting learning and retention of new information or concepts. In order to enhance learning, Ausubel believed that it is important for students to preview the information or concepts to be learned. For example, teachers can begin a

[16] Zone of Proximal Development, http://facultyweb.cortland.edu/~ANDERSMD/VYG/ZPD.HTML; How People Learn, http://www.nap.edu/html/howpeople1/ch4_b1.html

new topic with a brief introduction that provides an overview of the material about to be covered and relates this new material with what the students already know.[17]

In order to enhance learning, Ausubel believed that it is important for students to preview the information or concepts to be learned.

Implications for Instruction

This is just a small sampling of the various frameworks developmental psychologists have devised to understand and explain intellectual development. There are many others also worth studying, including Erik Erickson and John Dewey. You will find that there are recurring themes about learning that appear within many of these. At the same time, each theorist offers a different perspective on how learning, and the ability to learn, evolve. Viewed from that perspective, these theories offer evidence of the instructional and curriculum approaches that are most likely to facilitate successful learning. When you study these models, avoid thinking in rigid terms, particularly with respect to whether a student fits exactly as expected into a specific age category, or whether that student's development seems to be lagging. Rather, think about how the concepts discussed in these models can suggest ways for you to engage this student in learning, and instructional methods or approaches that can help all your students better understand the concepts you are trying to cover, or to master specific tasks.

The chart that follows (Figure 2.2) lists some of the main concepts of the developmental models discussed in this minicourse, along with information about what these concepts mean for the practice of teaching.

[17] "Meaningful Learning Mode" http://scied.gsu.edu/Hassard/mos/2.10.html; "Subsumption Theory" http://tip.psychology.org/ausubel/html; "Educational Psychology: David Ausubel" http://web/scuchico.edu/~ah24/ausubel.htm; "Advanced Organizers" http://chd.gse.gmu.edu/immersion/knowledgebase/strategies/cognitivism/AdvancedOrganizers.htm

DEVELOPMENTAL MODELS AND THEIR IMPLICATIONS FOR INSTRUCTION

Theory	Features	Implications for Instruction
Piagets' Theory of Cognitive Development	• Four sequential, age-related stages • The stages represent new abilities, not further development of original abilities. • A child must assimilate new information into existing cognitive structures.	• Educators must plan developmentally appropriate curricula that enhance students' logical and conceptual growth. • Teachers must plan lessons that take into account the roles that fundamental concepts, such as object permanence or conservation, play in a child's ability to learn. • Teachers must design lessons to build on existing knowledge and abilities. • Instruction should encourage interaction among peers.
Jerome Bruner	• Three relatively sequential stages of development • The stages build on one another and are progressively more complex. • Construction of knowledge is not done in isolation but rather within a social context.	• Effective curriculum must provide many opportunities and choices for students. • A variety of teaching approaches should be used to give students opportunities to construct knowledge in multiple ways. • Instruction must be structured so that the student can easily grasp it. • Instruction should be designed to facilitate extrapolation and/or fill in the gaps (going beyond the information given). • Instruction should be designed to take into account the student's cultural heritage and family background, particularly when learning is not progressing as well as might be expected.
Lev Vygotsky	• Culture teaches children what to think and how to think. • Full cognitive development requires social interaction. • Zone of Proximal Development	• The classroom and activities should be designed to foster group work and student collaboration. This will allow students to take on a teaching role with their peers as they master the skills at hand. • The teacher should interact with students, providing the minimum support necessary for students to engage with learning. The teacher should adjust the level of his or her help in response to each student's level of performance. The teacher needs to find a balance between supporting the student and challenging that student to reach beyond his or her current ability, and then encourage the student to act independently. • Assessment methods should take into account the Zone of Proximal Development and target both the level of ability or knowledge as well as the level of potential development.
David Ausubel	• Meaningful learning results when a student ties new knowledge to prior, relevant knowledge. • Advanced Organizer approach to teaching	• Learning materials should be carefully organized, presenting general ideas first, and then progressively differentiating them. • Instructional materials should attempt to relate new material with material that was covered previously. • New ideas and concepts should be meaningful to students.

Figure 2.2: Developmental Models

What mental models do students bring to your class and try to apply to the content you teach? What assumptions are their models based upon?

AGE-GROUP MILESTONES

Another way of looking at students is in terms of developmental milestones, which give a general idea about what to expect from children of different ages or in different grade levels. However, since children differ from one another in many ways and for many reasons, these milestones are best used as a guide, to help you design lessons and strategies appropriately. They can provide a way to keep track of what to expect—or not expect—from students in terms of learning style, physical and intellectual abilities, behavior, emotional control, social interactions, and so forth. You can use this information to monitor student progress and development, so that you can recognize signs that may indicate problems. In so doing, you will have a better chance to respond quickly, when necessary, by adjusting your lessons and strategies to help students reach their full learning potential.

These kinds of developmental charts can be quite extensive and may be broken down in greater detail. However, the simplified chart that follows can give you an idea of the type of the information you might use in your own investigation of age-group milestones. Further sources are listed in Appendix B.

ELEMENTARY SCHOOL STUDENTS	Students are eager to have the approval of adults.
	Students tend to exhibit an enthusiasm about learning new things that becomes contagious.
	Students are typically full of seemingly boundless energy and are learning how to be good students.
MIDDLE SCHOOL STUDENTS	Students are typically very concerned about what their peers think and do. They tend to wear, say, do, and value the same things their peers wear, say, do, and value.
	Students are in a constant state of change academically, socially, and emotionally.
HIGH SCHOOL STUDENTS	High school students are moving, at various rates, toward becoming adults. For many students, this is a time of struggling with an emerging personal value system, attempting to create a plan for their future, and weighing the value of ever-changing friendships.
	Having strong adult role models is important at this stage.
	School becomes the focal point for many students because it is the place where they may pursue their interests—academic, social, physical, and so forth. Some high school students spend nearly all their waking hours at school or doing school-related activities, while others find it a place with little relevance to their lives and either attend school sporadically or leave as soon as the school day ends.

LEARNING STYLE MODELS

As you observe your students participating in various learning activities, you are likely to notice that certain students seem to prefer learning a certain way while others are more comfortable learning another way. For example, a kindergarten teacher may notice that one student learns numbers more easily by counting objects, while another learns them by writing them down, and another by singing songs about numbers. Some students seem to thrive in noise and commotion, while others, if given a choice and the opportunity, will gravitate toward a quiet corner, and still others seem to be constantly engaged in conversation or daydreaming.

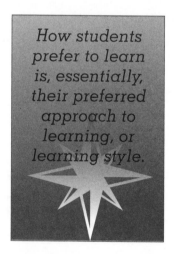

How students prefer to learn is, essentially, their preferred approach to learning, or learning style.

How students prefer to learn is, essentially, their preferred approach to learning, or learning style. That style may be influenced by a variety of factors, including a student's age, personal experiences, cognition, maturity, internal psychodynamics, and physiology. And, because the specific combination of these factors is different for each student, it stands to reason that each student will have a unique approach to how he or she perceives the world.[18]

Educational theorists have organized learning styles under numerous designations that focus on how students think, remember, or solve problems.

[18] O'Conner, Terry. Using learning styles to adapt technology for higher education. http://www.htctu.fhda.edu/prestools/ls/learning.html

These theories tend to focus on four general categories of learning preferences:

Instructional and environmental preferences. How environmental, emotional, sociological, and psychological preferences affect learning, such as preferences regarding physical setting (light, sound, temperature, classroom arrangement). These preferences can be tracked through observation, testing, and productivity studies.

Social interaction. How individuals behave in specific social contexts, such as the classroom.

Information processing. How information is obtained, sorted, stored, and utilized. Howard Gardner's Theory of Multiple Intelligences fits in this category.

Personality. How personality traits influence the way individuals relate to the world around them. The Myers-Briggs Type Indicators, which categorizes people as extroverts/introverts, thinking/feeling, sensing/intuition, and judging/perceiving, is a well-known personality model.[19]

In other words, learning style includes preferences for:

■ the type of information received

■ how students perceive information

■ how students organize information

■ how students process information

■ how students understand information[20]

Although these models look at learning style from different perspectives, they share a common message: Students will learn better when teaching accommodates their learning preferences and when they are given an opportunity to expand their preferences. Knowledge of your students' preferred approaches to learning enables you to plan and modify your teaching strategies and learning activities to accommodate your students' learning needs. It enables you to create educational experiences and modify teaching strategies and the classroom environment in ways that make learning more approachable, meaningful, exciting, and engaging for your students. For example, when planning learning experiences, this knowledge helps you choose instructional strategies and resources that enhance all students' engagement in learning, including interaction with each other and with the material. With this knowledge, an

> *Students will learn better when teaching accommodates their learning preferences and when they are given an opportunity to expand their preferences.*

[19] O'Connor, Terry. (n.d.). Using learning styles to adapt technology for higher education. Center for Teaching and Learning, Indiana State University. Web document available: www.htctu.fhda.edu/prestools/ls/learning.html
[20] Anderson, James. (March 2001). Tailoring Assessment to Student Learning Styles: A Model for Diverse Populations. *AAHE* Bulletin. Web document available: www.aahe.org/bulletin/styles.htm

accomplished teacher is able to design instructional activities and tasks that capitalize on individual student strengths and personal styles while, at the same time, helping them develop all areas of competence.

As is the case with developmental models, a full understanding of learning style models requires in-depth study. Although a comprehensive discussion of these theories is beyond the scope of this minicourse, this section of the minicourse introduces you to some of the more well-known models and offers a brief discussion of their main concepts. Additional resources that you can use for further study are listed in Appendix B.

GARDNER'S THEORY OF MULTIPLE INTELLIGENCES

Howard Gardner's theory of multiple intelligences suggests, as its name implies, that individuals have multiple intelligences—each to a varying degree. Gardner suggests that the traditional notion of intelligence, based on IQ testing, is far too limited and has more to do with the capacity for (1) solving problems and (2) fashioning products in a context-rich and naturalistic setting.[21] Instead, he proposes at least eight different intelligences[22] to account for a broader range of human potential in children and adults. These intelligences are:

Linguistic ("word smart"): The ability to use words effectively, whether orally (as a storyteller or public speaker, for example) or in writing (as a poet, journalist, novelist, editor, and so forth). These individuals exhibit a sensitivity to the meaning and order of words.

Logical-mathematical ("number/reasoning smart"): The ability to detect patterns, reason deductively, and think logically. These learners think conceptually in logical and numerical patterns making connections between pieces of information. Always curious about the world around them, these learners ask lots of questions and like to do experiments.

Spatial ("picture smart"): The ability to think in pictures, and to manipulate and create mental images in order to solve problems. This intelligence is not limited to visual domains—Gardner notes that children who are blind can have spatial intelligence.

Musical ("music smart"): The ability to understand and/or create music, and to perceive, discriminate, transform, and/or express musical forms. This ability includes sensitivity to rhythm, pitch or melody, and timbre of a musical composition. Musicians, composers, dancers, and music critics show a heightened musical intelligence.

---

[21] Armstrong, Thomas. (1994). *Multiple intelligences in the classroom*. ASCD: Alexandria, VA.
[22] Gardner himself points out that his model is tentative and that, after further research and investigation, some of the intelligences on his list may not meet the criteria he has set for defining what constitutes an "intelligence." It is also possible that he will identify *new* intelligences that do meet these specifications. These might include spirituality, humor, creativity, culinary, and intuition, to name just a few.

Bodily-kinesthetic ("body smart"): The ability to use one's whole body in a skilled way, to express ideas and feelings (as an actor, mime, or dancer) or toward a goal (as an athlete), or the facility to use one's hands to produce or transform things (as a craftsperson, sculptor, surgeon, or mechanic).

Interpersonal ("people smart"): The ability to perceive and understand others—their moods, intentions, feelings, desires, and motivations. This can include sensitivity to facial expressions, voice, and gestures as well as the capacity to discriminate among many different kinds of interpersonal cues, and to respond effectively to those cues. Political and religious leaders, skilled parents and teachers, and therapists are among those that use this intelligence.

Intrapersonal ("self smart"): The ability to be aware of one's own emotions, feelings, goals, and motivations and to have an accurate picture of one's own strengths and limitations; and the capacity for self-discipline and self-esteem.

Naturalistic ("nature smart"): The ability to easily recognize and classify plants, animals, and other things in nature. People such as farmers, ranchers, hunters, gardeners, and animal handlers may exhibit developed naturalistic intelligence.[23]

Key Points of Gardner's Theory

Gardner believes that all people possess these abilities to a greater or lesser extent. These intelligences function together in ways that are unique to each individual. Some individuals seem to be extremely capable in all or most of these intelligences while, at the opposite extreme, others appear to have only the most rudimentary aspects of the intelligences. Most people fall somewhere in the middle and tend to be highly developed in some of these intelligences, moderately developed in others, and relatively undeveloped in the rest (Armstrong, 1994). Gardner also suggests that virtually everyone has the capacity to develop each of these intelligences to a reasonably high level.

Gardner also argues that none of these intelligences exists by itself in real life (except, possibly, in very rare instances of individuals with brain injury or individuals with savant syndrome). Rather, these intelligences interact with each other in everything we do. Further, there are many ways to be intelligent within each of these eight categories. For example, a person may not be able to read or write but is a fantastic storyteller.

Gardner also recognizes that different cultures may emphasize different intelligences.

[23] Wilson, Leslie Owen. The eighth intelligence: Naturalistic intelligence. http://www.uwsp.edu/education/lwilson/learning/natintel.htm. Also, Resources in Teaching: Introduction to Multiple Intelligence Theory. http://www.harding.edu/~cbr/midemo/nat.html

Implications for Teachers

One of the exciting aspects of Gardner's theory of multiple intelligences is that it essentially provides teachers with "eight different pathways to learning" (Armstrong, 1994). If you are developing a unit of study, this theory suggests there are multiple approaches that can be effective in engaging all students. For example, if you are developing a science unit on insects for first-graders, you can include activities where students make insect puppets and create an insect play, draw diagrams of insects, move around pretending to be insects, explore insect habitats, and so forth.

> If you are developing a unit of study, this theory suggests there are multiple approaches that can be effective in engaging all students.

A complete discussion of Gardner's theory and its correct application to the classroom is beyond the scope of this book. Although Gardner has written that he does not believe that "there is a single royal road to an implementation of MI ideas in the classroom" (Armstrong, 1994, p. vii), he is also concerned about incorrect applications of his theory that have misrepresented the theory.[24] To avoid oversimplifying or misunderstanding Gardner's message, take time to review his works and those of some of the other resources listed in Appendix B. You can find more information in another PATHWISE Minicourse: *Designing Coherent Instruction*.

Collecting Information About Student Intelligences

There are various ways to collect information about student intelligences. However, many of the books written about this subject do not represent valid, reliable, or fair approaches to identifying intelligences. Talk to your school leaders and the families of your students before presenting a diagnostic exercise to your students. Keep in mind, also, that students are real people with complex and varying backgrounds and internal processes. And as such, they will not fit neatly into any one specific category or characteristic. In reality, they will reflect a combination of the various descriptions or categories presented in these models.

In addition to the models discussed in this minicourse, there are several other models worth investigating. When investigating any of these models, remember that it's not necessary to know each particular model in detail. Don't focus on the specific labels and categories. It's more important that you concentrate on understanding the major concepts they cover and how those concepts relate to your teaching practice. Remember, identifying learning styles is not about labels but about adjusting instruction to maximize individual student learning.

---

[24] Reflections on Multiple Intelligences: Myths and Messages in the Phi Delta Kappan, v. 77 n. 3, pp. 200-203, 206-209 (Gardner, 1995).

KOLB AND FRY LEARNING STYLE THEORY

David Kolb theorizes that all learners fall somewhere along two intersecting continuums, defined by their:

Ways of perceiving: Ranges from **Concrete Experience** (personal involvement and feelings) to **Abstract Conceptualization** (build theories, analyze)

Ways of processing: Ranges from **Active Experimentation** (application) to **Reflective Observation** (watch and ponder)

Kolb and Roger Fry (1975) argue that effective learning requires the possession of all four of these abilities (concrete experience abilities, reflective observation abilities, abstract conceptualization abilities, and active experimentation abilities). Further, they argue that people tend to develop a strength in (or orientation toward) one of these dimensions, rather than excelling in all four abilities. Hence, the Kolb and Fry learning style inventory (Kolb 1976) places people on a continuum between concrete experience and abstract conceptualization; and active experimentation and reflective observation.[25]

By knowing where a particular student lies in relation to these two continuums, a teacher can better target instructional strategies and learning activities to the individual student's learning needs.

In addition, Kolb's research found that individual differences in preferences for perceiving and processing information results in four different types of learners:

Diverger: The diverger learns intuitively through reflection. They are "big picture" people who work best when generating ideas, seeing situations from many perspectives, and organizing relationships into meaningful wholes. Imagination is their greatest strength (Krahe, 1993). These learners want to know how the learning material relates to them personally (their experiences, interests, and in the future).

Converger: The converger learns by thinking and then doing. They work best when systematically planning and logically analyzing ideas and finding solutions to problems. They are not "big picture" people but learn best when dealing in minute detail. Finding single answers to questions and practical applications are these learners' greatest strengths (Krahe, 1993). Scientists and engineers are convergers. They are good at carving out a problem from a greater whole and fixing it through experimentation. These learners like to understand how things work, and learn best in safe trial-and-error experimentation with stringent guidelines. They are doers who, in addition to experimenting, need to read and research. They also learn from lecture—if it is coupled with experimentation (Eubanks, 1997).

Assimilator: The assimilator learns by analyzing and reflecting. Assimilators are good at combining distinct factual observations into a meaningful explanation for a particular phenomenon. They can also make sure theories make logical sense. They are not into practical application as much as the abstract construction of theoretical models (Krahe, 1993). Theorists and college professors are examples of assimilators. Assimilators like to have their information presented in a highly organized format, and benefit from having time to think about the material. They also need time to reflect, but learn better from reading, researching, and listening to lectures (Eubanks, 1997).

Accommodator: The accommodator learns by doing what intuitively feels right. They are very flexible, adapting themselves to the specific and immediate circumstance. They learn best when they have a body of "experts" to draw from. They are best at exploratory and discovery learning (Krahe, 1993). The Alchemist of the Middle Ages is an example, mixing various substances to see what would happen. Today, teachers are probably the best example of accommodators, trying out new things with their children they think will work well. As learners, accommodators flourish under the least amount of constraint. Discovering through doing is how they learn best. You should assign them a broad learning task and monitor it to make sure they don't stray too far from your objectives, or do something unsafe (Felder, 1998). The accommodator not only requires hands-on experience, but also needs to talk about it at length.[26]

> When teachers are able to identify these learning styles in their students, they can better determine how to effectively teach those students.

When teachers are able to identify these learning styles in their students, they can better determine how to effectively teach those students. Kolb believes that learning styles are shaped by personality type and academic exposure. He believes that people who are naturally introverted are likely to also be reflective, and people who are extroverted will likely be action-oriented. He further postulates that school experiences shape learning styles in adulthood because teachers help to shape *how* people learn.[27]

[26]Kolb's Learning Styles, http://uwf.edu/coehelp/advid/cmatuszek/style/style.htm
[27]TRG Hay/McBer. (2001) http://trgmcber.haygroup.com/products/learning/lsius.htm

AN INVITATION TO REFLECT

Think about Kolb's description of a converger in relation to your curriculum and instructional delivery. How would a student who is strongly convergent fare in your classroom?

Figure 2.3 summarizes the four basic learning styles in the Kolb and Fry model.

KOLB AND FRY ON LEARNING STYLES (TENNANT 1996)		
LEARNING STYLE	**LEARNING CHARACTERISTIC**	**DESCRIPTION**
CONVERGER	Abstract conceptualization + active experimentation	• strong in practical application of ideas • can focus on hypo-deductive reasoning on specific problems • unemotional • has narrow interests
DIVERGER	Concrete experience + reflective observation	• strong in imaginative ability • good at generating ideas and seeing things from different perspectives • interested in people • broad cultural interests
ASSIMILATOR	Abstract conceptualization + reflective observation	• strong ability to create theoretical models • excels in inductive reasoning • concerned with abstract concepts rather than people
ACCOMMODATOR	Concrete experience + active experimentation	• greatest strength is doing things • more of a risk taker • performs well when required to react to immediate circumstances • solves problems intuitively

Figure 2.3: Kolb and Fry Learning Styles Model
Source: http://www.infed.org/biblio/b-explrn.htm

McCarthy's 4MAT System

Bernice McCarthy has developed a useful but complex teaching system called 4MAT, which focuses on teacher response to student learning profiles. Based on Kolb's work, and integrated with the work of other learning-style research, as well as recent findings in brain research, McCarthy describes four types of learners:

Type 1: Innovative Learners are primarily interested in personal meaning. They need to have reasons for learning—ideally, reasons that connect new information with personal experience and establish that information's usefulness in daily life. These learners seek to answer the question, "Why?" Some of the many instructional modes effective with this learner type are cooperative learning, brainstorming, and integration of content areas (e.g., science with social studies, writing with the arts).

Type 2: Analytic Learners are primarily interested in acquiring facts in order to deepen their understanding of concepts and processes. For these learners, the most important question is, "What?" They are capable of learning effectively from lectures, and enjoy independent research, analysis of data, and hearing what "the experts" have to say.

Type 3: Common Sense Learners are primarily interested in how things operate. They want to try things out for themselves. Type 3 learners want to know, "How does it work?" Concrete, experiential learning activities work best for them—using manipulatives, hands-on tasks, kinesthetic experience, and so forth.

Type 4: Dynamic Learners are primarily interested in self-directed discovery. They rely heavily on their own intuition, and seek to teach both themselves and others. These learners ask the question, "If?" Any type of independent study is effective for these learners. They also enjoy simulations, role play, and games.

McCarthy believes that all learners will be able to develop their own natural abilities when they are working in their own strongest learning style. At the same time, she believes to be successful learners, students must develop expertise in the other learning styles. She says students can become more proficient in these other learning styles by working in them. She argues that 25 percent of instruction should be devoted to each learning style, so that all learners receive instruction in their most comfortable style 25 percent of the time in the classroom. She also believes that learning has a natural cycle, beginning with Type 1 learning ("Why?") and moving sequentially through to Type 4 ("If?").

A 4MAT curriculum is designed so that all learning styles are addressed, so that students can both "shine" as well as "stretch." In other words, each lesson contains something for everybody, so each student not only works in his or her mode of greatest comfort, but is challenged to adapt to other less comfortable, but equally valuable, modes.[28]

---

[28] http://volcano.und.nodak.edu/vwdocs/msh/llc/is/4mat.html; See also Guild & Garger (1998), pp. 107-113, and Tomlinson (1999), p. 93.

Application to Teaching

To use 4MAT, you need to plan instruction for each of the four learning-type preferences on a given topic over the course of several school days. For example, some lessons would focus on mastery, some on understanding, some on personal involvement, and some on syntheses. This gives all your students a chance to participate in all four approaches so that each learner has a chance to approach the topic through his or her preferred mode, and also to develop strength in the areas that are "weaker."

To follow the 4MAT model, you begin by creating a learning experience and then offering students a way to analyze the experience personally. Then, the students integrate the experience and continue to analyze the new information in a more conceptual way, actually developing new concepts. Next, students practice with what is given, then make personal, practical application. They then synthesize by looking for something relevant and original. Finally, they seek to apply what they've learned to more complex experiences.[29]

For more information on the 4MAT system, explore the resources listed in Appendix B of this minicourse.

DUNN AND DUNN SYSTEM OF IDENTIFYING LEARNING STYLES

Rita and Kenneth Dunn's widely used system of determining and applying learning styles takes into consideration how physical setting, instructional materials, and classroom procedures affect learning. It is necessary to participate in professional development seminars to understand how to measure learning this system of identifying styles and how to apply that information to the classroom. The system is comprised of at least 18 learning style classifications organized in five preference areas: environmental, emotional, sociological, physiological, and psychological.

Using the Dunn and Dunn Learning Styles Model involves two steps:

1. Identifying individual learning styles using their Learning Style Inventory, which is available in three different forms: grades 3–5, grades 6–12, and adult (called the Productivity Environmental Preference Survey); and

2. Planning and implementing instruction to accommodate individual students' learning style strengths.

Once student learning styles have been determined through one of the inventories, in conjunction with observations, interviews, and tests, the teacher

---

[29] Guild & Garger. (1998). *Marching to Different Drummers*. ACSD: Alexandria, VA. p. 112.

can address the learning style of each student throughout the day. The system also provides information about common classroom patterns, which the teacher can use for adapting methods, physical environment, and groups. For example, the teacher can identify students who need quiet surroundings in order to learn, and those who prefer sound in the background.[30]

Like the other models in this section of Part II, the Dunn and Dunn system is quite complex and requires more explanation than can be provided here. To learn more, refer to the sources listed in Appendix B.

SUMMARY OF DUNN AND DUNN'S LEARNING STYLE ELEMENTS	
ENVIRONMENTAL STIMULI PREFERENCES	Sound Preference Light Preference Temperature Preference Design Preference
EMOTIONAL STIMULI PREFERENCES	Motivation Preference Persistence Preference Responsibility Preference Structure Preference
SOCIOLOGICAL STIMULI PREFERENCES	Self Preference Pair Preference Peers/Team Preference Adult Preference Varied Preference
PHYSIOLOGICAL STIMULI PREFERENCES	Perceptual Preference Intake Preference Time Preference Mobility Preference
PSYCHOLOGICAL STIMULI PREFERENCES	Global/Analytic Style Hemisphericity Preferences Impulsive/Reflective Preferences

Figure 2.4: Dunn and Dunn's Learning Style Model

[30] Guild & Garger. (1998), pp. 100-103. See also, The Dunn and Dunn Learning Style Model of Instruction, www.unc.edu/depts/ncpts/publications/learnstyles.htm

Learning style theories are guides for thinking about how your students might learn best. When used with caution and understanding, these theories can help you gain a better understanding of your students' learning preferences, which you can use to plan and modify your instructional strategies, approaches, and learning activities that support and enhance your students' ability to learn and grow. When using these theories, however, be careful not to over generalize about students. Doing so will work against your ability to build your knowledge of them as unique, ever-changing individuals.

> Learning style theories are guides for thinking about how your students might learn best.

AN INVITATION TO REFLECT

Do you have experience with McCarthy's or Dunn and Dunn's models? How do these models relate to the students with whom you work?

INVESTIGATIVE METHODS

"KIDWATCHING"

"Kidwatching," a term coined by Yetta Goodman (1978), refers to focused, purposeful observation of students in the act of learning. It's a technique that can reveal a wealth of information about students—information that often can't be learned through formal testing.

"Kidwatching" gives you a chance to pick up signs—some subtle and some quite obvious—of how your students are handling their learning experience. For example, an attentive kid-watching teacher can notice such things as confusion or understanding on a student's face. Through "kidwatching," you can also identify patterns of behavior, learning styles, and areas of strength or need. In addition, you can get a sense of your students' levels of motivation, interest, and oral and written language development. And you can observe how your students interact with peers, how they approach problems, and their

> "Kidwatching" gives you a chance to pick up signs—some subtle and some quite obvious—of how your students are handling their learning experience.

willingness to respond to questions either in a group or individually. From these observations, you can determine, for example, which students need extra help or specialized instruction.

You can "kidwatch" in many ways and in a variety of situations. For example, you can "kidwatch" while you circulate among students who are engaged in a learning activity. Or you can plan a "kidwatching" event. This might include scheduling a time to meet briefly with a student in a relatively quiet area of the classroom, while the rest of the class is busy. During this meeting you might have the student read for you, while you record ways in which the student's reading deviates from the actual text (a "running record"[31]). You might also use this time to discuss a specific piece of student work, such as a writing sample or math problem.

The time you spend in this interview session doesn't have to be long — a few minutes will do, if you know what you're looking for and carefully plan a series of questions or tasks that will provide you with the information you need. The session, although carefully planned, should be low-key and friendly. During such sessions, your students might reveal information beyond the specific learning issue at hand, such as a special interest or a source of anxiety. This information can go a long way toward adding to your knowledge of your students.

True "kidwatching" includes three steps[32]:

1. Observation

- What is the student's attitude toward the situation, task, or problem?

- What types of activities does the student seem to prefer?

- Does the student relate concepts to real-world situations?

2. Interaction... asking the student such questions as:

- What are you exploring? What are you reading?

- What information do you need to know to solve this problem? How can you get this information?

- What do you think will happen next? Can you tell me more?

- Have you discussed this problem (or this book/reading) with anybody else? Will you tell me about that discussion?

---

[31]A running record is a method for mapping a student's reading performance. As the student reads, the teacher records errors, self-corrections, hesitations, re-readings, repetitions, and requests for assistance. For more information see http://www.us.edu/newreading/runrec.htm or http://www.readinga-z.com/newfiles/levels/runrecord/runrec.html
[32]www.union-city.k12.nj.us/curr/preschool&K/assesment/p471.html

3. Analysis

■ What types of materials does the student read? What task or problem is he or she exploring?

■ Are the students' retellings, summaries, or reading/tasks sequential in nature? Is attention given to pertinent details and concepts?

■ Is the student's vocabulary or conceptual knowledge growing?

■ How does the student behave during periods of transition?

Finally, you want to keep a record of what you have observed, using such tools as checklists, time sampling, running records, or case studies.[33]

Although it is beyond the scope of this minicourse to fully explore the details of effective "kidwatching," it is a skill well worth developing. Additional resources that you can use for further study are listed in Appendix B.

INFORMAL OBSERVATION

Another, less formal but still very useful way to gather information about your students, is through informal observation. Watching interactions (or lack thereof) among students — emerging pecking orders and independent activities, for example — provides essential information about the way students learn and behave among their peers. You can watch how students interact with one another during study hall or lunch; what their behavior reveals during these unstructured times can be very informative. Which students are interacting with peers, and which seem to be somewhat isolated? Does one student in particular seem to be taking on a leadership role among the other students? What are the students who are not socializing doing? These are just a few things you can observe that may be relevant to in-class behavior and learning.

In addition to watching them while engaged in learning, Thomas Armstrong recommends observing students' "misbehaviors." He suggests that how students "misbehave" is a metaphorical indication of how they learn: the strongly linguistic student will be talking out of turn; the highly spatial student will be doodling; the bodily-kinesthetic student will be fidgeting, and so forth (Armstrong, 1994, p.28).

PARENT SURVEYS

Parent[34] surveys help parents communicate what they know about their child. They also let parents know that you are interested in finding out about the many aspects of their child, not just academic skills. When you send surveys to

---

[33] Case studies are real-life problems that students must solve. They can also be used to explore interpersonal relationships.
[34] The term "parent" refers to any adult caregiver who assumes responsibility for nurturing and caring for a child.

parents, you will find that you are more likely to get a timely response if you include a brief cover letter asking the parents for feedback about their child, explaining your purpose, and asking them to return the survey by a specific date (usually within the week).

Sample questions:

1. Does your child have a favorite TV show? What is that show?

2. Does your child interject opinions into discussions, tell jokes or stories, or initiate conversations? Describe the type of verbal interchanges or activities your child seems to enjoy engaging in.

3. Does your child like music? If so, what kind?

4. Describe a special talent or skill that your child is proud of.

5. What is the thing your child is most interested in right now?

6. What is the biggest change your child has made in the past year?

7. What would be your child's "dream future"?

8. What important things do you want me to know about your child?

9. List any concerns you have for the upcoming school year.

10. What goals do you have for your child this school year?

STUDENT INTEREST SURVEYS AND INVENTORIES

This type of survey encourages students to think about their interests, feelings, likes and dislikes, and share that information with you. Interest inventories and surveys can provide you with information about your students' interests and backgrounds.

Sample sentence starters:

1. If I could go anywhere, I would go _____.

2. When I am with my friends I feel _____.

3. My favorite song is _____.

4. In my free time I _____.

5. My number one goal is _____.

6. I like to read books about _____.

7. My most prized possession is _____.

8. I am most concerned about _____.

In what ways have you involved students' families or other adults in gathering information about students? What has been the result?

STUDENT RECORDS

You may find any of the following types of student records helpful, but they may not be available for all students.

- **Report cards** from previous years can be used to identify academic patterns or deviations from patterns of academic performance. Often, they also include some information regarding the behavioral and social aspects of the student.

- **Records from previous schools** can provide important information about patterns of performance and behavior in the classroom. If you are reviewing records that came from another school district, it is also worthwhile investigating the academic expectations and culture of that school.

- **Standardized test scores** can help you determine levels of achievement in comparison with national averages and with students within the school district. This information can help you identify students whose scores are either very high or very low, and give you a chance to investigate the implications of those scores. For example, students whose scores are at either extreme of the scale may need to be challenged at a higher level or they may need additional support. Standardized test scores can also reveal areas of skill that may make learning a particular discipline more difficult. For example, low reading and writing scores may make it harder for a student to learn a foreign language.

> **NOTE:**
> - Not all teachers understand how to read and interpret standardized test scores. If you find that you are not sure what all of the percentages and levels mean, be sure to check with an administrator in your school who can assist you with this part of your information gathering.
>
> - Standardized tests momentarily isolate specific skills and are just one source of information about a student's academic achievement. A summative judgment about performance or ability should not be based on a single measurement.

- **Individualized Education Plans (IEPs)** are designed for students who have been recommended for special education services. If you have students in your class who have an IEP, you should review it before planning instruction or assessment techniques because the IEP often requires that teachers use specific instructional or assessment approaches. The IEP also outlines any areas of difficulty that have been identified for the student, and recommends ways of addressing these areas. IEPs are legal documents and teachers must understand and follow them.

NOTE:

Implementing the required adaptations outlined in an IEP can range from giving a student unlimited time on an assessment to changing the assessment method completely. For example, you may only be permitted to use oral assessments for a particular student, as opposed to the written assessments you may be using with the majority of your class. Many IEPs now indicate that students must learn in an "inclusion class," which means that the additional support of a special education teacher is required within a regular education classroom. Understanding the extent to which the inclusion students need assistance from the special education teacher and the classroom teacher is important information for both teachers to discuss. The special education teacher and the classroom teacher must work closely together as they plan for the instructional and assessment choices that will be made for the inclusion students as well as the whole class.

- **Diagnostic testing results** may be included in a student's file. This information, if available, can identify a student's strengths and areas in need of support or development. You can use this information to individualize lessons accordingly.

- **Reports from experts**, which are sometimes found in student files, can be very important sources of information. These might include evaluations by psychologists, medical doctors, counselors, or educational consultants. These reports may include suggested strategies for best educating the student or offer explanations for particular behaviors.

NOTE:

Student files and records are confidential. Check school and district policies regarding access to this information.

PEOPLE

Family members, physicians, social workers, psychologists or counselors, as well as your own colleagues can offer perspectives and insights about students to which you may not otherwise have access.

- **Colleagues** may have had experience(s) with the students you are now teaching, or they may know the students' families. Informal discussions with colleagues can often help you to better understand your students' current behaviors and achievement.

- **Administrators** often have knowledge about students gained over time. They may know families and siblings, which may shed light on the current questions you may be attempting to answer about your students. They also have access to student files that can be helpful in determining patterns of behavior and/or learning.

I was teaching a student who understood the content, yet kept failing my assessments and never completed her homework. I spoke to her on a number of occasions, but she offered no rationale for her behavior. I then contacted her mother, who was also unable to explain why her daughter was doing so poorly. I then became very concerned because this student clearly understood the material but was failing my class. It was not until I was able to review her records via the principal's office that it became obvious that the onset of the problem coincided with her parents' divorce. I discussed this with the guidance counselor. Together we decided that the guidance counselor should have an informal conference with the student to see if this was what was bothering her. As it turned out, she was very eager to talk about it and her parents. Private counseling was arranged. Her grades and behavior improved over the school year once she was able to address her concerns.

- **Guidance counselors** often have established relationships with families and other supportive adults who foster growth in students. Children can have supportive but complicated relationships with the adults who care for them. Guidance counselors are sometimes better equipped to gather pertinent information about a student and then share it with teachers so they can better understand the student's needs.

- **Families** are sometimes difficult to connect with, but when the connection is made they can provide you with important information about their child. It is essential that parents know that you see them as your partners in the education of their child. If possible, it is also very important that your first contact with them be about getting to know their child, and not for disciplinary concerns. A survey for parents or significant adults to complete about their child is often enlightening for you and fun for them.

- **Students** themselves can provide revealing information about their motivations, concerns, and difficulties. Depending on their ages, students often appreciate being addressed directly and want to explain their educational needs and negotiate resolutions to problems in the classroom. You may want to set aside time to chat with them privately. At the beginning of the school year, as a way to help them introduce themselves to you, you may opt to ask them to fill out a "Getting to Know You" questionnaire, like the one that follows. Be sure to adapt the questionnaire to suit the grade level you teach.

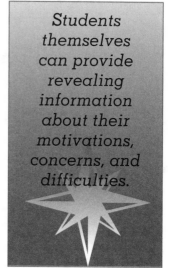

Students themselves can provide revealing information about their motivations, concerns, and difficulties.

Sample "Getting to Know You" Questionnaire

Name_____

What do you expect to learn in this class?_____

What experiences have you had outside of school where you have used this subject in everyday experiences? _____

What are your favorite classroom activities (example: group work, projects, speeches)? _____

What kinds of class activities do you like least (written exercises, games, hands-on activities)? _____

What activities or hobbies in and out of school are you involved in?

_____

On the lines below, please explain anything you feel I need to know about you in order to make your experience in my class a positive one.

_____

Sample "Getting to Know You" Game

Spends hours on the phone	Loves to read	Likes to hang out in his or her room
Listens to jazz	Acts in plays	Plays an instrument
Asks lots of questions	Loves math	Sings in the shower
Likes to run	Plays soccer	Speaks another language

Above is an example of a game that can be used to encourage students to mingle with the teacher and with each other. The game requires students to complete a grid that includes descriptions of people. Each box must be signed by someone who fits the description within the box. Students must mingle and ask questions of one another and the teacher in order to determine who can sign each part of this grid. The first student to fill in all 12 boxes with 12 different signatures wins. The real goal, however, is to help you begin gathering information about your students (their interests as well as how they interact) while they are getting to know each other. You may wish to adapt this game so that it gathers specific information for which you are looking or so that it relates to knowledge of skills specific to the content you teach.

OTHER TOOLS

- **K-W-L-Q charts** (Ogle, 1996) are a good way to help students connect with prior knowledge when beginning a new unit of study. Students are first asked what they **KNOW** about the new topic to be studied. Next, they share what they **WANT** to know about the new content. As students learn and explore new content, their questions can be used to stimulate new learning. After new learning takes place, students are asked what they have **LEARNED** about _____ (student question/topic being studied). As a way of continuing exploration, the chart has a final section for **QUESTIONS** students may still have about the new content.

- **Pre-tests and post-tests** can be used to determine the knowledge a student has in a specific subject area before and after a lesson or unit is taught.

- **Academic games** are often used by teachers to make learning fun. Framing learning activities as games allows the teacher to observe students in a different way within the classroom. Games can be focused specifically on getting to know students (especially appropriate at the beginning of the school year) and providing them with a chance to get to know each other as well.

- **Student interviews.** Using this technique gives your students a chance to tell you about their own learning. In addition to (or instead of) simply talking with your students, you can also ask them to write you a letter about their learning, outlining what they have learned about a particular unit or what they hope to learn about an upcoming unit. Or you might ask your students to complete written surveys to give you some insight into both their in-school interests as well as interests outside of the classroom.

Before beginning a unit in poetry, an eighth-grade teacher has students play a game. The students work in groups of four, and each group receives an envelope containing the text of a poem cut into its individual words (usually 30 to 40 words). Their goal is to create poetic phrases that can be arranged into a new poem. They have limited time to work, which forces them to work together and talk about what poetic phrases are and how to organize words. While they are playing the game, the teacher has an opportunity to walk around, observe, and listen to what is happening in each group. This gives the teacher a chance to establish whether these students seem to be interacting with their peers in ways that are considered appropriate for their age (age-group characteristics), how much they know about writing poetry (skills), and how they work within the group (learning styles).

AN INVITATION TO REFLECT

Take a few minutes to review the various investigative tools that have been discussed in this last section. What investigative tools do you currently use in your classroom to learn more about your students? List them below and briefly explain how you use each of them.

INVESTIGATIVE TOOLS CHECKLIST

Use the following checklists to identify the resources you will use when collecting information about the two students in your investigation. Decide who you need to speak with, what records you need to review, including where you will need to go or who you will need to contact to obtain these records, and what other Investigative Tools you will want to use. List this information on the checklist, along with the date by which you intend to have collected the information. Complete a separate checklist for each of the two students selected for focus. These checklists will allow you to quickly organize the information you have collected into a reference chart that you can use later on.

Student A: _____

People	Date
☐ Colleagues	
☐ Guidance counselors	
☐ Administrators	
☐ Social worker	
☐ Nurse	
☐ Psychologist	
☐ Other educational professionals	
☐ Family members	
☐ Coaches	
☐ Student	
☐ Other	

Records

☐ Previous report cards	
☐ Portfolios	
☐ Standardized test scores	
☐ Individual Educational Plans (IEPs)	
☐ Cumulative records	
☐ Diagnostic tests	
☐ Reports from experts	
☐ Other	

Investigative Tools	Date
☐ Interest inventory/survey	
☐ Learning-style inventory/survey	
☐ Conference with student	
☐ Conference with parents or other adult caregiver who assumes responsibility for nurturing and caring for this student	
☐ "Kidwatching"	
☐ Informal observations	
☐ Games/classroom activities	
☐ Assignments	
☐ Pre-tests and post-test	

Other Resources	Date
☐	

_____

Student B: _____

People   **Date**

☐ Colleagues
_____

☐ Guidance counselors
_____

☐ Administrators
_____

☐ Social worker
_____

☐ Nurse
_____

☐ Psychologist
_____

☐ Other educational professionals
_____

☐ Family members
_____

☐ Coaches
_____

☐ Student
_____

☐ Other
_____

Records

☐ Previous report cards
_____

☐ Portfolios
_____

☐ Standardized test scores
_____

☐ Individual Educational Plans (IEPs)
_____

☐ Cumulative records
_____

☐ Diagnostic tests
_____

☐ Reports from experts
_____

☐ Other
_____

Investigative Tools   **Date**

☐ Interest inventory/survey
_____

☐ Learning-style inventory/survey
_____

☐ Conference with student
_____

☐ Conference with parents or other adult caregiver who assumes
responsibility for nurturing and caring for this student
_____

☐ "Kidwatching"
_____

☐ Informal observations
_____

☐ Games/classroom activities
_____

☐ Assignments
_____

☐ Pre-tests and post-test
_____

Other Resources   **Date**

☐
_____

The following table (Figure 2.5) provides a handy summary of the Investigative Tools discussed in Part II. You will want to use it as a quick reference as you move through this minicourse.

SUMMARY OF INVESTIGATIVE TOOLS	
INVESTIGATIVE TOOL	INFORMATION ABOUT...
DEVELOPMENTAL MODELS: — PIAGET'S STAGES OF CHILDHOOD DEVELOPMENT — BRUNER'S THEORY OF CHILDREN'S COGNITIVE DEVELOPMENT — VYGOTSKY'S ZONE OF PROXIMAL DEVELOPMENT — AGE-GROUP MILESTONE MODELS	• characteristics of age group • students' varied approaches to learning
LEARNING STYLE MODELS — GARDNER'S MULTIPLE INTELLIGENCES — KOLB AND FRY — 4MAT — DUNN AND DUNN	• students' varied approaches to learning
FORMAL OBSERVATION INFORMAL OBSERVATION	• students' varied approaches to learning • students' skills and knowledge • students' interests and cultural heritage
INTEREST INVENTORIES AND SURVEYS	• students' interests and cultural heritage
RECORDS: — REPORT CARDS — RECORDS FROM PREVIOUS SCHOOLS — STANDARDIZED TEST SCORES — IEPs — RESULTS FROM DIAGNOSTIC TESTING — REPORTS FROM PHYSICIANS, COUNSELORS, EDUCATION CONSULTANTS	• students' skills and knowledge • students' varied approaches to learning • students' interests and cultural heritage
PEOPLE: — COLLEAGUES — GUIDANCE COUNSELORS — ADMINISTRATORS — FAMILY MEMBERS — STUDENTS THEMSELVES	• students' skills and knowledge • students' varied approaches to learning • students' interests and cultural heritage
OTHER TOOLS: — PRE-TESTS AND POST-TESTS — GAMES — ASSIGNMENTS	• students' skills and knowledge • students' varied approaches to learning • students' interests and cultural heritage

Figure 2.5: Summary of Investigative Tools

THE INVESTIGATIVE PROCESS FOR BUILDING KNOWLEDGE OF STUDENTS

Gathering accurate, comprehensive, and useful information that enhances your knowledge of your students in a way that is both efficient and effective requires careful planning. You need to make sure the information you gather is both accurate and relevant, that you can correctly interpret that information, and that you can appropriately and consistently apply what you have learned when planning and implementing your curriculum and instruction, as well as your instructional strategies and assessment methods. To help you in this endeavor, we have developed an "Investigative Process for Building Knowledge of Students," which is illustrated in Figure 2.6. This Investigative Process has been designed to help you gather the information you need efficiently, systematically, and purposefully. It is meant to be used over time, to support and enhance (1) your knowledge of your students as it relates to teaching and learning, and (2) your application of this new information to ongoing instruction and curriculum development.

> This Investigative Process has been designed to help you gather the information you need efficiently, systematically, and purposefully.

This Investigative Process is the process you, the teacher, will use as you go about developing your knowledge of your students. Using this process, you will (1) decide what you need to know and about which students, (2) select and use your Investigative Tools to gather this information, (3) interpret what the information you have gathered tells you about your student(s), (4) apply that information to your instructional practice to effectively meet the individual learning needs of your students, and (5) assess outcomes and plan next steps. This cycle is similar to the PATHWISE Minicourse Learning Cycle, which is the learning cycle you are following as you work through this minicourse and incrementally advance your teaching practice — in this case, in becoming skilled in the concept and application of the framework for teaching component, "Demonstrating Knowledge of Students."

To begin the process, you need to become thoroughly familiar with the four elements that comprise the "Demonstrating Knowledge of Students" framework component. These elements systematically describe and define the various aspects of students' personalities, abilities, and background that affect how and what they learn.

After you understand these four elements, you will need to develop a working knowledge of the various tools (we call them "Investigative Tools") that can help you gather learning-relevant information about your students, and decide which of these tools are more likely to extract useful information for each specific element. There are many Investigative Tools at your disposal—some you will feel more comfortable with and will be more in keeping with your teaching style than others. Some are more informative than others, depending on the teaching-learning situation. Some you might find relatively complicated, while others will be easier for you to understand and work with. Which Investigative Tools you choose, however, will depend more on the information you need to elicit than on how comfortable you are in using them. Therefore, it is critical that, once you've determined which tools are appropriate for the task at hand, you take the steps that are necessary to fully comprehend how these tools work and to know how to use them effectively.

Once you have gathered this information about the four elements, it will be time for you to apply it to the Investigative Process. In the meantime, it's important to have an idea of the process now, so you can begin thinking about how you will be using this new learning later, when you begin to apply it to your practice. This will help you put your learning into perspective.

SUMMARY OF THE INVESTIGATIVE PROCESS

The first step of the Investigative Process—**Identify**—begins with selecting the student(s) for focus during your investigation. Next, you identify the rationale, goal(s), and questions to be addressed. This leads you to determining the elements of "Demonstrating Knowledge of Students" that best fit with your stated rationale, goal(s), and questions. Finally, you select the Investigative Tools that will best support your investigation.

The second step—**Gather Information**—gives you the opportunity to use your identified Investigative Tools to collect information about your selected student(s) and elements. With information collected, you move to the third step—**Interpret Information**—where you sort, analyze, and use the collected information to develop a working understanding of your student(s) in relation to the elements that have been used to structure the investigation.

In the fourth step of this process—**Apply New Understanding**—you apply your developed knowledge base to curriculum design, instructional planning and strategies, and assessment to make your students' learning experiences more interesting, relevant, accessible, and engaging.

Finally, as you integrate your knowledge of your students into your teaching, you will want to collect evidence that you can use to evaluate your performance in the Investigative Process and the influence your new knowledge has had on student learning. In the fifth step—**Assess Progress and Plan Next Steps**—you will decide, what, if any, additional steps you will take.

THE INVESTIGATIVE PROCESS FOR BUILDING KNOWLEDGE OF STUDENTS

STEP 1: IDENTIFY

As you begin your investigation, identify

- Student(s) selected for investigation

- Your rationale, goal(s), and/or questions for the investigation

- Element(s) to be explored:

  — Characteristics of the age group

  — Students' varied approaches to learning

  — Students' skills and knowledge

  — Students' interests and cultural heritage

- Appropriate Investigative Tools

STEP 2: GATHER INFORMATION

Use selected Investigative Tools to collect information about identified

- Student(s)

- Element(s)

Step 3: Interpret Information

Interpret the gathered information to determine students'

- Individual strengths and interests
- Cultural heritage
- Cognitive, emotional, and/or social development
- Learning styles

based on selected elements for investigation

Step 4: Apply New Understanding

Apply the knowledge base to develop or revise approaches to effectively meet individual learning needs via

- Curriculum design
- Instructional planning and strategies
- Assessment methods

Step 5: Assess Progress and Plan Next Steps

Collect and interpret evidence of student progress and plan for next steps.

Figure 2.6: The Five Steps of the Investigative Process

Directions: The following activities are intended to help you explore the investigative tools presented in Part II. The activities should be completed

	COMPLETED
2.1 a. Select one of the *developmental models* discussed in Part II (refer to Figure 2.5) with which you would like to become more familiar. Using any of the resources cited in Part II, Appendix B, or resources of your choosing, read more about the model (at least two articles or book chapters). Reflect on what you have read, recording your responses to guiding questions in **My Minicourse Journal** which follows. b. Select one of the *learning style models* discussed in Part II (refer to Figure 2.5) with which you would like to become more familiar. Using any of the resources cited in Part II, Appendix B, or resources of your choosing, read more about the model (at least two articles or book chapters). Reflect on what you have read, recording your responses to guiding questions in **My Minicourse Journal** which follows.	
2.2 Think about the two students you selected for focus in Part I. How might you apply the models you selected for further reading to better understand Students A and B? Using the **Information I Want to Gather** chart that follows, develop lists of questions for each student relevant to the two models — developmental and learning style — you have been studying. For example, if you chose Kolb and Fry's learning style model, your list might include questions like, "Does Student A have an emotional reaction to learning?" or "Is Student B a risk-taker?"	

	COMPLETED
2.3 Review the section in Part II on student-interest and parent surveys. Using the provided samples in this section, develop your own questions or modify sample questions to create student-interest and parent surveys to help you better understand your students from the perspectives of their families and of the students, themselves. Each survey should include eight to ten questions. Your surveys should be recorded in the **Designing Surveys** section that follows.	
2.4 Review the section on "Kidwatching" in Part II. The more you use this investigative tool, the more information it can provide about your students. To start practicing this skill, begin with one of the two students you have selected for focus during this minicourse. Select a learning situation where you can informally observe this student, interact with her or him, and then analyze what you have learned from watching this student in the act of learning. Use the **"Kidwatching"** chart that follows to identify the learning situation, and then summarize anecdotal notes taken during the observation and interaction, collected evidence of student learning, new information learned, and application of this new information.	
2.5 **The Investigative Process — Step 1: Identify.** For each student selected for focus, you will be conducting an investigation to learn more about the student. You will be following the Investigative Process steps outlined in this minicourse and completing an **Investigative Process** chart, which follows, for each student — Students A and B. At this point in the minicourse, you are ready to begin working on Steps 1 and 2 of the Investigative Process, using the **Investigative Process — Part 1** chart as follows:	

a. **Elements, Goals, and Rationale:** Identifying goals for an investigation is one of the first sub-steps of Step 1: Identify. These goals should be specific and measurable and should relate to one or more elements of the component, "Demonstrating Knowledge of Students." You may want to relate your goals to Activity 2.2 or you may want to work through other priorities.

Use the first column for each **Investigative Process — Part 1** chart to record the element(s) related to each investigation. (It may be easier to record your goals first, and then determine which element(s) are related to each goal.) Using the second column of the **Investigative Process — Part 1** charts, record your investigation goals for the two students selected for focus, as well as your rationale for conducting each investigation, as appropriate. In other words, what concerns or issues do you want to address? What do you want to learn about this student and why? What do you see as the objectives for completing this investigation?

Try to have at least one goal for each of the four elements. In some cases, you might find that several elements comprise a goal you have set. In that case, record all of those related elements in the Elements column. Most likely, you will continue to revisit, add to, and modify this chart as you continue through this minicourse.

NOTE:

You may find that you have both long-term and short-term goals. In that case, identify them as such. What is most important is to record your thoughts and document your work as you move through the Investigative Process so that you can reflect on them later.

b. **Questions to Answer:** Identify the questions you want to answer as they relate to your goals, using the third column of the **Investigative Process — Part 1** chart. These questions will help guide the next steps of your investigation. Again, you will most likely continue to add questions to this column as you move through this minicourse.

c. **Investigative Tools:** Identify the investigative tools you might use to progress to your goals. List these tools in the fourth column of the **Investigative Process — Part 1** chart.

NOTE:

Many of these tools may be new to you. Think of this investigation as an opportunity to start exploring new tools. Some you will find easier to learn and apply than others. You may find that you want to learn more about a tool before you actually try it. Use resources noted in Part II, Appendix B, or suggested by knowledgeable colleagues to learn more about these tools and their applications. Keep in mind that this minicourse is about developing and expanding your own professional skills in order to more effectively teach and connect with your students — so accept some of the uneasiness that accompanies trying something new, and know that you are working toward a more proficient practice.

d. **Identifying Observable Outcomes:** To complete Step 1 of the Investigative Process, complete the fifth column of the **Investigative Process — Part 1** chart by listing expected outcomes (tangible evidence) as a result of applying your new knowledge to effectively meet individual student needs. In other words, what will tell you that this new understanding has positively impacted a student's learning experience?

Refer to the sample **Investigative Process — Part 1** chart, which follows, as an example and guide.

2.6 **Investigative Process — Step 2: Gather Information.** Begin now to start using investigative tools to collect information that answer your questions recorded in Step 1: Identify. As you collect information pertinent to the goals, rationale, and questions you've identified, summarize and record this information in the right-hand column of the **Investigative Process — Part 1** chart. Refer to the sample chart, which follows, as an example and guide.

NOTE:

For now, leave Steps 3–5 in the **Investigative Process — Part 2** chart empty. You will complete these steps and this chart after completing Part IV of this minicourse.

2.7 If you are part of a study group, discuss your responses to Part II Related Activities as well as the material you have read. To help you recall what was said, take notes during the discussion using the **What I Learned from Other Resources** chart that follows.

RESOURCE	INPUT

INVESTIGATIVE PROCESS—PART 1
STUDENT: (SAMPLE)

	STEP 1: IDENTIFY				STEP 2: GATHER INFORMATION
ELEMENTS	GOALS/ RATIONALE	QUESTIONS TO ANSWER	INVESTIGATIVE TOOLS	OBSERVABLE OUTCOMES	SUMMARY OF COLLECTED INFORMATION
Skills and knowledge Interests Approach to learning	To increase Student A's engagement in science class, including class participation, completion of labs and other assignments, and overall effort. Student A does not seem to work to his level of ability.	What kinds of interests/hobbies does Student A have in and out of school? What is Student A's level of interaction and participation in other classes and settings? What is Student A's level of knowledge for a new science unit on light?	Student-interest survey "Kidwatching" Pre-test Other teachers Family survey Learning style models	Student A will participate more in class and small-group discussions. Student A will complete all class, lab, and homework assignments in an accurate, thorough, and timely manner.	In a student interest survey, Student A expressed interest in photography including developing his own pictures. Submitted a photograph he took to the school newspaper. Member of the after-school photography club. Rarely talks in either whole-class or small-group settings unless given a specific written direction or prompt. Pre-test on light unit indicates a good level of understanding of basic concepts.

STEP 3: INTERPRET INFORMATION	STEP 4: APPLY NEW UNDERSTANDING		STEP 5: ASSESS PROGRESS AND PLAN NEXT STEPS
INTERPRETATION OF INFORMATION	IMPLICATIONS FOR INSTRUCTION AND ASSESSMENT	ACTION TO BE TAKEN	EVIDENCE OF LEARNING
Student A has a strong interest in photography that might be transferable to the classroom. Socially interacts through this medium. Good understanding of science concepts, but needs concrete direction to share his knowledge and skill. Tends to be a divergent thinker, using both concrete experiences and material and his creativity to see things from multiple perspectives — good problem solver when able to focus on tangible resources and clearly stated objectives.	For required science unit on light, Student A could study how a camera works and its relationship to light — then share this knowledge with peers. Photography could be used for a science project where Student A creates a portfolio of photography representing concepts being taught in class.	Check-out books on cameras and photography Design science lab dealing with photography and light Develop assessment giving students the option of using photography to demonstrate understanding of light. (e.g., Photography portfolio)	On (date) Student A asks/responded to 5 whole-class and small-group questions; high level of interaction with peers for 30 minutes. Student A conducts a demonstration for the class on light and photography, explaining how a camera works. Uses photography for a culminating project, creating a photo portfolio that explains how light played a part in each photo taken. Student A volunteers to be the "class photographer" documenting the class year through photography. Completes all homework assignments and earns high marks on lab reports.

my minicourse
Journal

Developmental model: _____

1. Why did you select this model?

2. Summarize the key ideas from your reading:

3. In what ways can you use this developmental model to learn more about your students?

4. How do you plan to apply this new learning to your practice?

5. What questions do you still have about this developmental model? How might you go about answering these questions?

Journal

Learning style model: _____

1. *Why did you select this model?*

2. *Summarize the key ideas from your reading:*

3. *In what ways can you use this learning style model to learn more about your students?*

4. How do you plan to apply this new learning to your practice?

5. What questions do you still have about this learning style model? How might you go about answering these questions?

Developmental model: _____

Questions related to Student A:

Questions related to Student B:

Learning style model: _____

Questions related to Student A:

Questions related to Student B:

USE THIS SECTION TO DEVELOP STUDENT-INTEREST AND PARENT SURVEYS THAT WILL HELP YOU BETTER UNDERSTAND YOUR STUDENTS' INTERESTS, GOALS, AND DREAMS.

Student-Interest Survey

Parent Survey

Student: _____

a. Select and describe a learning situation to informally observe:

b. Develop questions to ask to determine the student's level of engagement in this learning setting:

c. Summarize anecdotal notes taken during the observation and interaction:

d. Explain what you have learned about this student in this learning setting from reviewing your notes and evidence of learning, such as student work completed during this learning activity.

e. Identify how you plan to apply this new learning to teaching this student?

INVESTIGATIVE PROCESS — PART 1 STUDENT: A					
STEP 1: IDENTIFY					STEP 2: GATHER INFORMATION
ELEMENTS	GOALS/ RATIONALE	QUESTIONS TO ANSWER	INVESTIGATIVE TOOLS	OBSERVABLE OUTCOMES	SUMMARY OF COLLECTED INFORMATION

STEP 3: INTERPRET INFORMATION	STEP 4: APPLY NEW UNDERSTANDING		STEP 5: ASSESS PROGRESS AND PLAN NEXT STEPS
INTERPRETATION OF INFORMATION	IMPLICATIONS FOR INSTRUCTION AND ASSESSMENT	ACTION TO BE TAKEN	EVIDENCE OF LEARNING*

* Whenever possible, record specific data—exact words, frequency, assessment results, and/or attach artifacts.

Elements	Goals/ Rationale	Questions to Answer	Investigative Tools	Observable Outcomes	Summary of Collected Information
Step 1: IDENTIFY					**Step 2: GATHER INFORMATION**

STEP 3: INTERPRET INFORMATION	STEP 4: APPLY NEW UNDERSTANDING		STEP 5: ASSESS PROGRESS AND PLAN NEXT STEPS
INTERPRETATION OF INFORMATION	IMPLICATIONS FOR INSTRUCTION AND ASSESSMENT	ACTION TO BE TAKEN	EVIDENCE OF LEARNING*

* Whenever possible, record specific data — exact words, frequency, assessment results, and/or attach artifacts.

NOTES

PART III

- UNDERSTAND HOW TO USE INCREASED KNOWLEDGE OF STUDENTS TO PLAN MORE EFFECTIVE INSTRUCTION AND ASSESSMENTS.

FILTERING THROUGH GATHERED INFORMATION

It can't be said often enough: How students think and learn, and how they respond to learning in general as well as to specific learning situations has everything to do with who they are and where they come from. Each student is born with a unique predisposition for learning in certain ways, and each is also a product of external influences, including his or her immediate family, extended community, and culture.[35] Each has his or her own range of interests, passions, skills, and knowledge base. Each comes from a different socioeconomic background, which may, among other things, affect that student's access to books, computers, and cultural experiences. And each will have a unique upbringing; for example, some students have parents who encourage debate and inquiry, while others come from a background where such activities are discouraged. Some will come from an urban environment, others from the suburbs, and still others from rural communities. Some will have had earlier experiences in different schools that had traditions, rules, and expectations that may or may not have been similar to those of their current school. All of these factors will come into play when these students enter your classroom.

Knowing this is the first step toward being prepared to accommodate the myriad of differences among students, and toward being better equipped to create learning experiences that your students will find exciting, relevant, and engaging. With this understanding, you can begin to use some of the Investigative Tools, including the Organizational Models and the Investigative Methods discussed in Part II — or any other valid investigative approach not covered in this minicourse — to purposefully and thoughtfully gather information about your students.

Once you have collected this information, your next step is critical — you filter through the information you have gathered about your students in a sensitive, nonjudgmental, and unbiased way, to determine how this information can help you modify your

---

[35] Guild, P.B. and Garger, S. (1998). *Marching to Different Drummers*. Association for Supervision and Curriculum Development: Alexandria, VA.

current instructional practices in ways that will help all your students achieve their full potential as learners. As you examine the information you have gathered about your students, be careful not to make simplistic inferences about your students' cultural or socioeconomic backgrounds—much variation exists in both! Think deeply and with an open and educated focus. Otherwise, it will be far too easy to make naïve, inappropriate (perhaps even offensive) teaching decisions.

An Invitation to Reflect

What personal biases or preferences do I need to explore?

Likewise, train yourself not to make assumptions based on outward appearance or behavior. For example, don't assume, simply because a student wears an extreme hairstyle or eccentric clothes, that this student lacks the interest or motivation to learn, or that the student's only interests are those of the peer group with which he or she is outwardly identifying. You may find, for example, that this student is extremely well read for his or her age, or that he or she is a talented classical musician. Similarly, a student who is jumpy, distracted, impulsive, or acting out in class may not have a "learning disability." That student may, in fact, be reacting to problems at home, to an allergy, or simply because he or she is bored and unable to engage in learning in the way it is being presented.

> Think deeply about the behavior you observe and the information you gather in your investigation.

In other words, don't jump to conclusions. Think deeply about the behavior you observe and the information you gather in your investigation. Weigh and balance each item of information you have collected against the others, and against any other aspects of this student's situation you know about. Ask yourself, for example, if something is happening in world events that might affect the student's ability to focus on daily lessons. Is something happening in the school or classroom that might disrupt learning, such as noisy construction or tension among certain groups of students? Is there a problem at home? In the community? Does the student have medical issues? Is the student currently involved in an athletic endeavor or pursuit of some other activity that might be affecting the student's ability to engage in learning? Is there some way you can take this information and turn it around so that it is no longer an obstacle to learning but can be used to engage the student in learning?

Once you have carefully thought through these questions and come to some conclusions about what this information tells you about your students, you can begin to modify your instructional approaches and strategies in ways that will enhance your students' ability to engage and learn.

THINKING ABOUT YOUR OWN TEACHING STYLE

As you are thinking about your students, also keep in mind that you, too, have your own personal background, cultural heritage, interests, passions, and ways of approaching problems and sorting through information. When you begin to use your new-found knowledge of your students to modify your instructional approaches and strategies, you will want to be aware that you will be more comfortable using certain approaches, and less comfortable with others. Although you may initially choose to use approaches with which you are comfortable and familiar, eventually you will want to challenge yourself to use new approaches to address the learning needs of your students. This should be more about expanding your repertoire with techniques and strategies that complement your own strengths, rather than attempting to change your personal teaching style. For example, although you may be highly sequential, you can intentionally invite students to do things out of sequential order by offering opened-ended time during the day.[36]

You may also find it enlightening, both for yourself as well as your students, to share some of this information about yourself with your students. Let them know that you have a passion for mysteries or for a particular type of music; tell them you tend to assimilate information better if it's presented graphically rather than in words. In addition to helping your students realize that their teacher is also a real person, this information may help them feel more comfortable about their own individuality and perhaps help them understand why you use some of the approaches you use. It might even empower them to feel free to remind you that they might need to have things explained differently or that they need to approach new knowledge from a different perspective.

AN INVITATION TO REFLECT

As a learner, did you ever have to change your approach to learning in order to understand challenging content or to master a new skill? Describe the experience.

[36] Guild, P.B. and Garger, S. (1998). *Marching to Different Drummers*. Association for Supervision and Curriculum Development: Alexandria, VA.

CONSIDERATIONS FOR USING KNOWLEDGE OF YOUR STUDENTS TO INFORM YOUR PRACTICE

Once you have analyzed the information you have gathered, you can begin making decisions about how and when to use that information in your daily classroom practice. Think carefully about when it will be appropriate to vary your classroom methods, to use new types of materials, to offer a range of assignment choices, or to modify your assessments. Ask yourself which changes are appropriate and constructive, and which are not.

As you begin making these decisions, it's important to remember that the goal isn't to add variety for variety's sake, but to offer choices that reflect the specific learning needs of your students.

As you begin making these decisions, it's important to remember that the goal isn't to add variety for variety's sake, but to offer choices that reflect the specific learning needs of your students. For example, if you are going to offer students a range of assignment choices, make sure those choices take into account your students' interests, current knowledge level, and learning approaches.

And once you begin to implement these changes, be sure that you do not emphasize the strategy over the ultimate learning goal. For example, you may decide to use phonics, which is a teaching strategy, to help your students become more proficient readers. However, if a student has not been successful in learning with the phonics approach, change strategies for this student — it's not necessarily essential that the student master phonics at this moment, it's essential that he or she becomes a proficient reader. Similarly, a student who learns best through hands-on activities may become disruptive or inattentive during a typical linguistic type of lesson. Rather than immediately labeling that student as a troublemaker or as having Attention Deficit Disorder and continue in the same mode, consider providing more time for hands-on learning opportunities.

You may find it easier to stay on track by repeatedly asking yourself the following questions:

- What outcomes do I expect from this approach?

- What are my overarching learning goals for my student(s)?

- Based on my knowledge of the student(s), what changes should I make if the student(s) does not seem to be succeeding through the approach I've chosen?

- How can I use my knowledge of this student (these students) to make the most appropriate and helpful educational decisions?

GATHERING IDEAS FOR NEW TEACHING STRATEGIES

Learning new approaches and strategies, and applying these strategies effectively and appropriately, is an essential part of developing a student-focused approach to instruction. This process begins with developing an accurate, perceptive, informed knowledge of your students based on your own valid and unbiased investigation of those students.

There is no one right or wrong way to go about learning different approaches and strategies. You can get ideas by watching and working collaboratively with other successful teachers who use approaches that are different from the ones you currently use. Or you can delve in the wide range of publications that address various teaching strategies and approaches; many of these are listed in Appendix B. A full discussion of specific approaches and strategies is beyond the scope of this minicourse, but consider extending your study through two other PATHWISE Minicourses: *Engaging Students in Learning* and *Designing Coherent Instruction*.

For the purposes of this discussion, however, the most important point to bear in mind is that your use of these diverse approaches should be based on your well-informed knowledge of your students' specific learning needs. The choices you make when determining which approach or strategy to use should be made thoughtfully and judiciously, with a clear understanding of your students' individual strengths, abilities, and learning preferences, and individual learning needs.

USING KNOWLEDGE OF STUDENTS TO DEVELOP A STUDENT-FOCUSED APPROACH TO TEACHING

Recognizing, honoring, and accommodating each student's individual learning needs is essential if we are to achieve equal access to education for all learners in today's classrooms. As Pat Burke Guild and Stephen Garger point out in *Marching to Different Drummers*, fair and equal access to education implies equal opportunity, which may require different (i.e., unequal) approaches. To accommodate the diverse population of students who enter today's classrooms—students with different needs, different backgrounds, different access to opportunities and experiences—teachers must develop a deep

> *Recognizing, honoring, and accommodating each student's individual learning needs is essential if we are to achieve equal access to education for all learners in today's classrooms.*

understanding of their students' individual learning styles, cultural heritage, and the entire range of elements that comprise "Knowledge of Students." Based on this knowledge, teachers can then find meaningful, effective ways to apply this knowledge to their teaching practice.

Teachers who have taken the time to get to know their students are able to accommodate a myriad of differences among those students and are better equipped to create exciting, engaging learning experiences for those students. Furthermore, when teachers provide learning experiences at levels students can understand, that build on what they already know, that accommodate their preferred learning styles and interests, and are challenging but not overwhelming for them, students are more likely to enjoy learning, to persevere even when learning doesn't come easily, and to initiate learning on their own. And, if these students can then demonstrate their newly acquired understanding through an assessment that is appropriate for their individual readiness level, learning preferences, and interests, they are more likely to be able to show what they have learned.

> **Teachers who have taken the time to get to know their students are able to accommodate a myriad of differences among those students and are better equipped to create exciting, engaging learning experiences for those students.**

Students who can connect with a teaching style or assessment approach usually become more confident in their own abilities to learn and perform. This confidence improves their motivation to learn, achieve goals, and succeed on assessments—often far beyond original expectations.

Learning happens when students are able to connect new information to what they already know, and when they can see how this new information applies to their lives. There are many instructional approaches that teachers can use to help students make these connections. Two of these—**differentiated learning and cooperative learning**—are particularly appropriate for this discussion because, to be successful, they both require that the teacher develop a deep and well-researched knowledge of their students' interests, abilities, level of learning preferences and needs. And at the same time, when used with thought and understanding, they can also advance the knowledge you have already ascertained about your students.

DIFFERENTIATED INSTRUCTION

Differentiated instruction is a student-focused approach to teaching that recognizes and responds to students' varying abilities, background knowledge, readiness, language abilities, learning preferences, and interests. In differentiated instruction, teachers use a variety of instructional and assessment strategies in an effort to accommodate their students' individual learning styles, readiness levels, interests, and personal characteristics while, at the same time, maintaining high expectations for all students in the class.

Once you understand that all learners differ in terms of readiness, interests, and learning approach, you can work toward a classroom—a differentiated classroom—in which everybody works to master essential understandings, knowledge, and skills, although they use different processes, different content, different materials, and different products to get there. The intent is to maximize each student's growth and individual success—regardless of ability, readiness level, or individual learning needs—by meeting each student where he or she is, and assisting in the learning process. By capitalizing on students' individual interests, this personalized approach to instruction encourages students to become more invested in learning. As a result, they often exceed the learning goals originally set for them by their teacher.

The intent is to maximize each student's growth and individual success ... by meeting each student where he or she is, and assisting in the learning process.

Several of the key characteristics of differentiated instruction are specifically relevant to this discussion of developing knowledge of students and using that knowledge to maximize student learning. These include:

- The teacher and students accept and respect one another's similarities and differences.

- The teacher begins where the students are (so must *have knowledge* of where the students are), and recognizes that students differ in important ways.

- The teacher modifies (or personalizes) content, process, and products to attend to these individual differences.

- The teacher provides appropriate ways for each student to learn as deeply as possible and as quickly as possible.

- To do this, the teacher uses a variety of instructional strategies and materials to help target instruction to student needs.

- The teacher understands and balances group and individual norms.

- The teacher begins with a clear understanding of what constitutes powerful curriculum and engaging instruction, and then asks what it will take to modify instruction so that each learner comes away with understandings and skills that prepare them for the next phase of learning.

- All students are given the opportunity to participate in work that is challenging, meaningful, interesting, and engaging for each of them.

- Classroom time is used flexibly in the sense that pacing is varied according to individual and group needs.

- Students work in a variety of group configurations, as well as independently.

- Students are often given the opportunity to choose the topics they wish to study, ways they want to work, and how they want to demonstrate their learning.

- Students and their teacher collaborate in setting class and individual goals.

- Students are assessed in multiple ways, and each student's progress is measured at least in part from where that student begins. Assessment is an ongoing diagnostic activity that guides instruction. Learning tasks are planned and adjusted based on assessment data.

- The teacher is primarily a coordinator of time, space, and activities rather than a provider of information. The aim is to help students become self-reliant learners.

- The teacher functions as a diagnostician who prescribes the best possible instruction for each student.[37]

According to Carol Ann Tomlinson, author of *The Differentiated Classroom: Responding to the Needs of All Learners*, three elements of curriculum can be modified, based on the teacher's knowledge of his or her students: content, processes, and products.[38]

Content is what you want your students to know (facts), understand (concepts and principals), and be able to do (skills), as well as the means through which that learning is accomplished (e.g., textbooks, supplementary readings, demonstrations, field trips, computer programs). When using a differentiated approach, you need to align tasks with your instructional goals and objectives. Your instructional concepts should be broad-based, rather than focused on minute details or unlimited facts. The instructional content should address the same concepts with all students, but it should be adjusted to accommodate the diverse learners in your classroom.

For example, if your learning goal for a particular math lesson is for students to be able to determine the area of a rectangle, you might present the problem as a "word problem" for some students. For students who have difficulty with word problems, however, you might present the problem using pictures or diagrams. You might ask other students to construct a rectangle using pieces from a Tinkertoy® construction set, tongue depressors, or similar manipulatives, and then fill it with blocks. Regardless of which method the students use, each is able to achieve the same learning.

[37] Tomlinson, C.A. (1999). *The Differentiated Classroom: Responding to the needs of all learners*. ASCD: Alexandria, VA.
[38] Tomlinson, *The Differentiated Classroom...*; Also, Wehrmann, Kari Sue. (September 2000). Baby steps: A beginner's guide (The journey to a differentiated classroom starts with small steps). *Educational Leadership* (58)1. www.ascd.org/readingroom/edlead/0009/wehrmann.html

Processes are the activities students use to make sense of essential ideas and information (the content). These are typically activities designed to let students process ideas and information on their own, rather than having it presented to them by a teacher or in a textbook, for example.

One of the most successful strategies used in differentiated classrooms involves **flexible ability grouping**. Flexible ability grouping assumes students have different levels of ability and understanding, depending on their prior knowledge of the topics or their current levels of skill. Students are expected to interact and work together as they develop knowledge of new content. You may conduct whole-class introductory discussions of content "big ideas" followed by small-group or pair work.

You might organize these groups based on your students' individual readiness, learning styles, or interests, for example. The important thing to remember is that ability levels vary for each student, so that a student may need to be in one group for math, another for language arts, and so forth. Grouping and regrouping should be a dynamic process; movement out of and between groups should depend on when a student reaches a new level of ability, not when the content changes.

> Grouping and regrouping should be a dynamic process; movement out of and between groups should depend on when a student reaches a new level of ability, not when the content changes.

Another approach is to hold **classroom clinics** on any topic with which students are having difficulty or need more time to study. With this approach, you invite students to attend the clinic to improve skill in a specific area. While you are conducting the clinic, other students continue to work independently, or in centers, stations, or groups. Clinics may be as specific as working on understanding the proper use of commas in a prose essay or regrouping in math, or they may cover broad concepts, such as elements of style in literature. You can also ask student groups to conduct clinics for other groups in areas that they have studied in depth.

> Imagine a forum held in support of a civics-related social studies learning standard. In this forum, different student groups explain their varied political platforms to other class members. One day, half the class presents, while the other half acts as the audience; the next day, the class reverses roles.

Many teachers who differentiate instruction employ **tiered learning** structures. In this method, you address the same concepts and skills with all your students, but you vary the assignments in terms of complexity, abstractedness, and open-endedness, depending on the individual student's particular learning needs. You can assign the varied activities, or you can let your students pick the one that challenges them or speaks to their interest or learning style. The goal is to ensure that students of varying learning needs work with the same essential ideas and use the same key skills, but they learn concepts and constructs at varying levels of depth and complexity. In addition to accommodating a variety of learning styles, tiered learning can help busy students balance their workloads. When asked to select a challenging activity, a student might instead request a less consuming but still instructive assignment if there are other major projects looming, or if the student is involved in a music or sports event that is currently demanding a lot of his or her outside time and energy. By having a choice of assignments, students have an opportunity to be more reflective and autonomous. Most students will not "take advantage" of the situation, because they will gravitate toward assignments that pique their interests, or fit their learning style.

> *The goal is to ensure that students of varying learning needs work with the same essential ideas and use the same key skills, but they learn concepts and constructs at varying levels of depth and complexity.*

There are a host of other tried and true strategies you can use to differentiate instruction. The following list, adapted and condensed from *The Differentiated Classroom: Responding to the Needs of All Learners*, by Carol Ann Tomlinson, gives a brief overview.

- **Stations.** Using stations involves setting up different areas in the classroom where students work on various tasks simultaneously. These stations invite flexible grouping because not all students need to go to all stations all the time.

- **Compacting.** This strategy encourages teachers to assess students before beginning a unit of study or development of a skill. Students who do well on the pre-assessment do not continue work on what they already know.

- **Agendas.** These are personalized lists of tasks that a student must complete in a specified time, usually two or three weeks. Student agendas throughout a class will have similar and dissimilar elements.

- **Complex instruction.** This strategy uses challenging materials, open-ended tasks, and small instructional groups. Teachers move among the groups as they work, asking students questions and probing their thinking.

- **Orbital studies.** These independent investigations, generally lasting three to six weeks, revolve around some facet of the curriculum. Students select their own topics and they work with guidance and coaching from the teacher.

- **Entry points.** This strategy from Howard Gardner proposes student exploration of a given topic through as many as five venues: narrational (presenting a story), logical-quantitative (using numbers or deduction), foundational (examining philosophy and vocabulary), aesthetic (focusing on sensory features), and experiential (hands-on).

- **Problem-based learning.** This strategy places students in the active role of solving problems in much the same way adult professionals perform their jobs.

- **Choice boards.** With this strategy, work assignments are written on cards that are placed in hanging pockets. By asking a student to select a card from a particular row of pockets, you can target work toward student needs yet allow student choice.

- **4MAT.** Teachers who use 4MAT plan instruction for each of four learning preferences over the course of several days on a given topic. Thus, some lessons focus on mastery, some on understanding, some on personal involvement, and some on synthesis. As a result, each learner has a chance to approach the topic through preferred modes and also to strengthen weaker areas.

Products are the vehicles through which students demonstrate and extend what they have learned and can do as a result of a considerable segment of learning. Products reveal whether students can apply learning beyond the classroom to solve problems and take action. You can ask students to create different products based on their individual readiness levels, learning preferences, or interests, for example. By differentiating products, you give students the opportunity to demonstrate to the best of their ability what they know, what they have learned, or what they can do.

Products reveal whether students can apply learning beyond the classroom to solve problems and take action.

For example, as a culminating product for a unit on the Middle Ages, one student might choose to give an oral presentation to show what he or she has learned about the influences of music on social policy in the Middle Ages. Another student might opt to play an instrument and act out the various ways that music influenced social policy in the Middle Ages. Both students can show increased knowledge and understanding of this topic, but through two very different forms of assessment. Another way to differentiate a product is to give students a choice of working alone on the product, or working in a group.

This type of strategy requires the teacher to have a clear understanding of assessment criteria for each type of project (and to communicate that criteria to his or her students), as well as knowledge of students.

MAKING DIFFERENTIATION POSSIBLE IN YOUR STUDENT-FOCUSED CLASSROOM

As mentioned earlier, the first step in being able to differentiate instruction is to know your students—their current levels of achievement, learning styles, skill levels, interests, and backgrounds. This knowledge will give you the information you need to design meaningful, student-focused instruction and assessment.

> Making the transition to differentiated instruction is best accomplished in small steps and over time.

Making the transition to differentiated instruction is best accomplished in small steps and over time. Rather than attempting to completely recast your classroom practice, only make a few changes at a time, focusing on doing them as well as possible. Set reasonable goals for yourself, and stick with them. Teachers—like their students—grow best when they are moderately challenged, but not overwhelmed. You can begin to experiment with differentiation by adding student choice to a previously teacher-directed lesson or unit.

For example, in a unit about authors' techniques for showing character development, you ask students to choose and read one of six novels selected by their teacher. The goal is for the students to understand that dialogue is an effective way to reveal characters within a novel. Let's assume you have chosen six novels based on their clear use of dialogue to show character development, and the likelihood that your students will find them engaging. Rather than assigning a particular novel to each student (a more traditional approach), you let the students choose which one they want to read. In this way, the novel becomes the vehicle through which students achieve the goal for this portion of the unit and, because these novels address the goals for this unit, your goal is met. At the same time, your students have been given a chance to choose novels they believe will be most interesting and engaging for them.

You can also differentiate instruction by tapping into the interests of your students. In so doing, you can make learning both exciting and relevant.

For example, in a lesson about predicting weather patterns, you can ask students what it is about weather patterns that interests them, and then use that information to let the students personalize their study of weather. You can let students predict weather for any time or place that is of interest to them, provided that you have explained the criteria by which you will be assessing the predictions. They can predict whether or not they will be able to play outside on a particular day, play softball on the weekend, or enjoy a day at the beach—or whether they can anticipate enjoying a day in the snow, instead of in class. All of the students will be learning about how to predict weather based on weather patterns, but they will be doing it for a personal reason, which makes this new-found knowledge more meaningful to them.

To make this approach successful, however, you need to develop an assessment strategy that lets your students hand in specialized predictions, rather than perform identical work on a test that doesn't acknowledge the students' individual interests. Another simple way of differentiating instruction is to provide a range of activities or assessments from which students can choose.

For example, let's assume you are teaching a unit on reading and notating music, and your goal is to determine whether students can identify and define standard notation symbols for pitch, rhythm, dynamics, tempo, articulation, and expression. You might assess your students through one of three methods: conventional testing (matching, fill-in-the-blank, or multiple choice), visual representations, or written descriptions. At the beginning of the unit—after you have presented rubrics or guidelines for each type of assessment—you can have each student choose which assessment type he or she prefers. In this way you can measure learning while also allowing students to select the mode of presenting their new understandings that best fits their learning styles.

Over time, you will become more comfortable with this new approach to teaching and assessing. You will be able to design entire units in this way, because differentiation is a matter of creating different pathways to reach the same understanding. Many teachers gradually add more differentiation to their instruction each year, and eventually their classrooms revolve around student choice and varied assessment techniques. Moreover, when done correctly, differentiated instruction coordinates teachers' knowledge of their students with the state, district and/or teachers' learning goals. You can differentiate instruction during a single unit of study or as a yearlong practice.

GROUP LEARNING

In cooperative learning, students of different ability levels are placed together in small groups and assigned specific learning activities, which the group is expected to complete. Each group member has a role to fill in completing the activity, and each member of the group is responsible not only for his or her own learning but also for helping others in the group learn. By working in small groups, students can share strengths and also develop their weaker skills.

Although the possible variations for cooperative learning grouping is practically unlimited (you can vary the group's size, the group's function, and the types of roles the group members play, for example), most involve small groups of students (typically, three to five) of varying talents, abilities, and backgrounds. These heterogeneous groups work together on a group task in which each member is individually accountable for part of an outcome that cannot be completed unless all the members work together. The teacher or the group assigns each team member a personal responsibility that is essential to successful completion of the task.

In order for cooperative learning to be successful, care must be taken when assigning students to a group. Students must be grouped appropriately so that each student's individual strengths and abilities enhance, compliment, and support those of the other group members. Because members of a cooperative learning group take on various roles and responsibilities within the group, thought must be given to who to assign to which group, as well as to which roles or responsibilities are appropriate for each student. This, of course, means that, in addition to having a clear understanding of what you want to accomplish, you need to have a well-developed knowledge of your students—their abilities, their learning-style preferences and learning needs, their personality quirks (the leaders, the followers, the clock-watchers, for example), how they tend to react when working in groups, and their interests.

> *Students must be grouped appropriately so that each student's individual strengths and abilities enhance, compliment, and support those of the other group members.*

Many teachers who plan to implement a cooperative learning approach spend the first weeks of school getting to know their students by observing them as they interact with one another and as they participate in various learning activities, including whole-class learning, small-group learning, independent work, collaborative problem solving, and so forth. This period of observation, or "kidwatching," gives you a chance to learn about your students' differing strengths, areas of need, personalities, how they tend to interact with peers as well as authority figures, their level of confidence, and their individual interests. In addition to observing your students, you might want to employ one or two other Investigative Tools discussed in Part II in order to gather specific information about your students for the purpose of making more informed decisions when developing groups.

GROUPING CONSIDERATIONS

When creating cooperative learning groups, you will want to consider some of the following student characteristics:

- academic skills and ability levels
- gender
- cultural heritage
- race/ethnicity
- family background
- socioeconomic background

- social skills
- level of self-confidence
- level of motivation
- leadership skills
- learning needs and preferences
- interests, hobbies, and passions

AN INVITATION TO REFLECT

What types of information (that are not readily apparent through observation) would you like to gather about your students in order to develop effective cooperative learning groups?

As mentioned earlier, careful consideration must be given to which students to assign to a particular group, as well as to the role each student will play within the group. Clearly, students who are skilled in areas that are necessary for a group's success can become the group's strongest members, which gives them an opportunity to be group leaders. But what about students whose abilities and skills are less obvious? How do you assign roles that give these students a leadership role? By gaining a deeper knowledge of your students' skills, interests, and abilities, you will be able to make these decisions wisely. A sensitive teacher who knows more about his or her students than what is immediately apparent can use that knowledge creatively to give *each* student a chance to play an important, meaningful part in the group's overall success. For example, in your middle school or high school class, you might notice a student who is good about seeking the opinion of shy students, mediating differences of opinion among peers, breaking down problems into smaller steps, translating words or concepts described in research material into everyday language, organizing ideas or people, or drawing visual representations.

> A sensitive teacher who knows more about his or her students than what is immediately apparent can use that knowledge creatively to give *each* student a chance to play an important, meaningful part in the group's overall success.

NOTE:

Group learning is particularly suitable when focusing on students' various learning styles or multiple intelligences because they can be structured to include students representing each of the different styles or intelligences. For instance, a group charged with the task of plotting recent earthquakes might include a socially developed student to help organize the group, a spatially developed student to plot the earthquake occurrences, a strongly linguistic student to write a report describing the group's observations, and so forth.

Some typical group roles include:

- **Facilitator.** This student uses interpersonal skills to help the group work together and keep on task. The facilitator makes sure that all members of the group have an opportunity to participate and learn, and that each maintains respect for their team members. She or he facilitates group decision making, makes sure each member of the group completes his or her task, and looks out for the overall success of the group. The facilitator may also be responsible for ensuring that all of the group members have mastered the learning points of a group exercise.

- **Fact Checker.** The fact checker makes sure that the group's work actually represents all of the efforts and opinions of all of the members of the group. He or she may also be expected to verify the accuracy of the information used by the group, as well as to make sure everyone understands the information or work expected of them.

- **Material Manager or Researcher.** This student locates, gathers, and returns (at the end of the group task) any information and resources the group needs for completing its work. If an activity has a strong research component, you may consider assigning this task to more than one group member.

- **Reporter.** The recorder documents all group activities, including the material contributed by each group member, group decisions, group discussions, and conclusions. He or she might write out the solutions to problems for the group to use as notes or to submit to the teacher. When needed, the reporter may also prepare and present the group's decisions, findings, opinions, or conclusions to the class either verbally or in a written report.

- **Timer.** The timer makes sure the group accomplishes its task(s) in the time allotted. Once the group determines its course of action, the timer helps the group set goals for accomplishing the work on schedule. He or she then monitors how well the group adheres to its schedule. The timer is also responsible for informing the teacher if the group has difficulty maintaining its schedule.

- **Monitor.** The monitor is responsible for making sure that the group's work area is left the way it was found.

- **Tutor.** The tutor provides assistance when other students in the group are having difficulty understanding content or applying skills.

- **Praiser.** This student praises the group for hard work and praises individuals for sharing, helping, listening, and checking.

- **Questioner.** This student acts as a go-between for the group when students are unsure of how to proceed. The questioner takes the group's questions or concerns to the teacher, or surveys other groups, to get answers to the group's questions.

- **Wildcard** (in groups of five). This student acts as an assistant to the group leader and assumes the role of any member that may be missing.

AN INVITATION TO REFLECT

What group roles are appropriate for the students and the content you teach? How can you use these roles to reinforce your students' strengths and to encourage individual growth?

A complete discussion of the intricacies involved in developing and implementing successful cooperative learning strategies is beyond the scope of this minicourse. However, another PATHWISE minicourse—*Engaging Students in Learning*—includes a deeper discussion of some of the many effective cooperative learning models you might want to use with your students. Other resources are listed in Appendix B of this minicourse.

ASSESSMENT

In this student-focused approach to teaching, assessment ranks as one of the most important Investigative Tools at a teacher's disposal. Through assessment, teachers can gather critical information for next steps in the teaching and learning cycle. At the same time, to effectively guide teaching decisions, assessment requires prior knowledge of student's current abilities, knowledge, learning preferences, interests, and learning needs.

ASSESSMENT AND THE STUDENT-FOCUSED CLASSROOM

In recognizing and embracing the notion that students learn in different ways, you also understand that, just as with learning approaches and strategies, assessment strategies should focus on students' individual learning needs. They, too, should be student-focused. This means:

Assessment should let students shine. That is to say, assessment should be designed and implemented in a way that permits students to show, to their best ability, what they really know and can do under the best circumstances—not under the worst or most stressful circumstances. This means that, just as with instruction, assessments should be engaging, accessible (both in terms of learning approaches as well as challenge), familiar, and (to the extent possible) take into account the individual student's approach to learning.

> This means that, just as with instruction, assessments should be engaging, accessible (both in terms of learning approaches as well as challenge), familiar, and (to the extent possible) take into account the individual student's approach to learning.

Let's face it, even in best-case situations, it's a rare student who actually finds assessment engaging, let alone a positive experience. (In most students' minds, it is safe to say, assessment is still "testing" and still equates to expectations and pressure.) For example, students who are given "boring" tasks or tasks they don't find relevant are likely to be too unmotivated or disinterested to produce the kind of work they are fully capable of producing. This can be just as true for very successful, motivated students as it is for students who are struggling with learning.

Assessment should come in a variety of shapes and flavors. No single form of assessment works well in all situations, nor for all students and all purposes. Some will fit certain assessment goals and situations better than others. Some students will perform better on one type of assessment than another. Some will shine in individual performance situations, while others are more comfortable working in groups. Consequently, students should be given the opportunity to show competence in any one of a variety of ways.

Limiting yourself to using only one or two assessment methods, no matter how tried-and-true, limits your ability to fully understand the range of your students' knowledge and skills. Conversely, providing students with different kinds of opportunities to show what they know will give you a broader, better understanding of each student's individual talents and abilities. At the same time, it exposes students to different assessment methods, giving them more opportunities to demonstrate their skills and knowledge.

Assessment should be ongoing, diagnostic, and linked to instruction. More than providing grounds for assigning a grade or ranking students, assessment's fundamental purpose is to provide evidence, to be informative, about what students know and can do, or how they are responding to particular learning situations—so that teachers can make good instructional decisions. It should be focused on helping students grow more than on cataloging their mistakes or ranking their place in a classroom.

Effective teachers constantly monitor and revise instruction plans based on their students' learning progress. Assessment, whether informal or formal, plays an integral part in this ongoing process, providing teachers with the evidence they need for determining whether or not their students have achieved the learning goals set out for them; their readiness to move on to new ideas, concepts, or skills; their interests; and how and in what situations they learn and process information best.

From this perspective, assessment is another Investigative Tool that you can use to help you understand (based on what it tells you about your students) how to modify future instruction to maximize your students' learning. The information garnered from this type of ongoing assessment can also help you match learning tasks to individual student needs. Such ongoing (i.e., *formative*) assessment might be in the form of pre-tests, homework assignments, whole-class discussions, journal entries, or interest surveys, to name a few. Even when administering end-of-chapter or end-of-course, summative-type assessment, you can still vary your assessment strategies so that each student can fully demonstrate his or her skills, level of knowledge, or understanding.

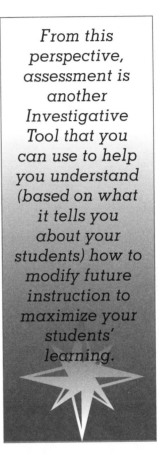

From this perspective, assessment is another Investigative Tool that you can use to help you understand (based on what it tells you about your students) how to modify future instruction to maximize your students' learning.

ASSESSMENT OPTIONS

Teachers have all sorts of options available to help them gather evidence about their students' learning or information about their individual interests, approaches to learning and problem solving, and the like. These range from the informal, day-to-day ways that teachers size up their students' progress (such as observation and questioning strategies) to traditional paper-and-pencil tests (multiple-choice and short-answer tests, for example) and inventories, to more elaborate forms of assessment, such as task-based performance assessments. Like a detective, you can use these Investigative Tools to gather the evidence you need to make wise educational judgments. And, like any good detective, you will use more than one source of evidence to ensure that you can accurately interpret the evidence to build a convincing case for modifying your instructional approaches.

Furthermore, like any good detective, you will study this information in the context of what you already know about your students. So, by having gained important, learning-relevant knowledge, you will be better equipped to understand what this evidence really means in terms of how your students are learning, and how you can best help them progress in that learning.

Tests. This is a broad category that includes unit pre-tests and post-tests, essay tests, and tests that require students to apply knowledge or skills. Tests can be modified to accommodate individual student needs in many ways, including varying the form of the test (oral vs. written, multiple-choice vs. essay) depending on the student's needs, allowing students to select a certain number of questions to answer, allowing students to take the test with a partner, giving the student extra time to take the test, providing word banks, and giving special consideration for errors in spelling, mechanics, and organization.

Performance Assessments. Unlike multiple-choice or true-false tests (which ask students to choose from among responses that are provided), performance assessments require students to perform a task or generate their own responses. Examples of performance assessments include written compositions, analysis or interpretation of a piece of literature or artwork, works of art, science projects, musical performances, speeches, open-ended math problems, to name just a few.

These assessments typically consist of two parts: a task and a performance criteria or rubric. Rubrics are critical in performance assessment for two reasons: First, scoring these complex forms of assessment fairly and consistently can be quite challenging. A rubric establishes clearly defined standards of performance and then provides exact guidelines describing what constitutes an acceptable response or performance. For example, if the task is an essay, the scoring guide should state a range for the number of supporting details necessary to achieve an outstanding score, an average score, and so on.

This scoring guide should be shared with students *before* they take the assessment. You should discuss the standards with your students to make sure they clearly understand the level of work expected for each criterion, and possibly even make student-suggested changes to the rubric—if those changes make sense in terms of the learning goals or standards being assessed. Studies show that involving students in discussing and developing rubrics helps them to more fully understand what is important about the performance or product. Besides being instructionally valuable, this kind of pre-assessment exchange often gains a higher level of student buy-in. Plus, students who are given a choice in the type of project to complete will often choose one that fits with their preferred approach to learning, which gives them a better chance to fully engage in the assessment and, as a result, give their best performance.

Individualized Assessments. Individualized assessments are often done by contract with a student. The student collaborates with the teacher to design an assessment that fits the student's strengths and meets the teacher's needs for determining mastery. Once the teacher and student agree on the assessment's design, they can draw up a contract outlining the teacher's expectations and the student's responsibilities. Individualized assessment also refers to when an existing assessment has been modified to address specific learning needs.

Stiggin's Model involves three "tools": Student-involved classroom assessment, student-involved record keeping, and student-involved communication. This model defines success as continuous improvement. It requires students to contribute to the criteria for their assessment (student-involved classroom assessment), which means that they self-evaluate as they are working to determine where they are in relation to the assessment goals. Because they have helped to define "success," it becomes more attainable. The next tool, student-involved record keeping, means that the student must monitor improvements over time, which builds self-confidence and becomes a motivator for future success. Lastly, self-involved communication, or being able to communicate success to important adults and peers in their lives, leads students to internalize their success and that prompts future success. This model allows students to control their learning and is based on the premise that success breeds success and motivates students to learn.[39]

COLLECTING AND EVALUATING WHAT YOU HAVE LEARNED

Whatever assessment approaches you choose to use, keep in mind that your ultimate goal is to gain more knowledge about your students — what they know, what they can do, whether they are ready for new learning, how they function within certain assessment environments — and to use that knowledge to modify or individualize your instructional practice to enhance student learning.

> By acknowledging and accommodating your students' differences as you choose your assessment strategies, you are preparing to give your students the opportunity to be fully engaged in the assessment and, as a result, to show you what they really know and can do.

Further, as with diversifying your instructional approaches or using cooperative learning, assessment is most effective and most informative when it takes into account the knowledge you already have of your students. By acknowledging and accommodating your students' differences as you choose your assessment strategies, you are preparing to give your students the opportunity to be fully engaged in the assessment and, as a result, to show you what they really know and can do. The next step, analyzing this information in the context of what you already know about your students, helps you to make the best possible instructional decisions for your students. With this information, you will be able to

---

[39] Stiggins, Richard. (November 1999). Assessment, student confidence and school success. Phi Delta Kappan.

match learning tasks to each student's individual needs, plan lessons that are sufficiently challenging but not too far over their heads, and choose materials that will encourage further learning.

AN INVITATION TO REFLECT

If you kept a record on individual students' success rates with different methods of assessment, what would it say about your assessment approaches? About your class's performance?

A complete discussion of assessment strategies and the principles of validity and reliability, and how to implement these strategies, is beyond the scope of this minicourse. You can learn more from the ETS publication: *Letting Students Shine: Assessment to Promote Student Learning* and *PATHWISE ONLINE: The Fundamentals of Classroom Assessment*, or by reviewing some of the resources listed in Appendix B.

Directions: The following activities are intended to give you the opportunity to explore your own style of teaching as well as student-focused instructional strategies. The activities should be completed sequentially and in a manner conducive with your personal learning style.

		COMPLETED
3.1	Part III discusses the importance of understanding one's own approach to and comfort with both learning and teaching. The reflective questions in this activity guide you in identifying your preferred approaches to learning and teaching. Use **My Minicourse Journal**, which follows, to record your responses.	
3.2	The deeper your understanding of new instructional and assessment strategies, the more likely you will be to try them in your classroom and add them to your teaching repertoire. To this end, select and review one or two articles/books on differentiated instruction. Use references noted in Part III, Appendix B, or another resource to help you locate reading material. After completing your reading, respond to the guiding questions located in the following space entitled **Review of Differentiated Instruction**.	

3.3 **Trying It Out.** The sooner you try out some of the differentiated instruction/assessment strategies you've been learning about, the more likely you will be to try out additional strategies and build on your growing knowledge of this important approach. For this activity, you will use an existing lesson/learning experience with which you are familiar and modify it from the perspective of differentiated instruction. If possible, you should videotape the implementation of this lesson in order to reflect on it later. Your focus for your reflection will be both the lesson's implementation and Students A and B. The following chart, **Trying It Out — Using Differentiated Instruction**, should be completed for planning and implementing this lesson.

3.4 After implementing your lesson/learning experience, use the space entitled **Reflecting on Implementation** to review your implementation, the evidence you collected, and what you've learned about differentiated instruction through this experience.

3.5 Continue to collect information about Students A and B, adding it to the **Investigative Process** charts in Part II Related Activities.

my minicourse
Journal

1. *Thinking about yourself as a student, how do you most prefer to learn? What learning style(s) and approach(es) to learning are most comfortable for you? Feel free to respond to this question from the perspective of one or more of the learning style models discussed in this minicourse.*

2. *Thinking about yourself as a teacher, what approach(es) to teaching feel most natural? What types of instructional strategies, grouping of students, and instructional materials do you find that you use most often in your practice?*

3. *What methods of assessment are you most comfortable using?*

4. *How do you think your own preferences and comfort level with various learning and teaching approaches affect your practice and your students?*

REVIEW OF DIFFERENTIATED INSTRUCTION

What experience have you had using differentiated instruction before beginning this minicourse? Explain your experiences, or, if this is a new approach to teaching for you, explain your initial thoughts when first reading about it in this minicourse.

SUMMARIZE THE KEY IDEAS FROM YOUR OWN READING:

RESOURCE(S):

SUMMARY OF FINDINGS:

How do you plan to apply this new learning to your practice? Be specific citing both instructional and assessment strategies you plan to try in your classroom.

What questions do you still have about differentiated instruction? How do you plan to go about answering these questions?

Trying It Out—Using Differentiated Instruction

Lesson/learning experience topic:

Standard(s) addressed:

Learning goal(s): (What specifically do you want students to know or be able to do as a result of this lesson?)

Differentiated instruction: (What strategies do you plan to use to make this lesson student-focused?)

Concepts

What concepts, facts, and/or skills are being addressed in this lesson?

What materials, resources, manipulatives, or other instructional aids are being used to support differentiated instruction?

PROCESS

What processes or activities do you plan to use to make this lesson student-focused (e.g., workstations, complex instruction, choice boards, classroom clinics)?

PRODUCT

What product(s) and other forms of evidence of learning will result from this lesson? How will students demonstrate what they have learned and what they can do? How are product expectations being differentiated to give students the opportunity to demonstrate their understanding and skill?

ADAPTATIONS

What lesson adaptations (if any) do you plan for your focus students in light of the four elements of "Demonstrating Knowledge of Students"?

ADAPTATION	STUDENT A	STUDENT B
AGE-APPROPRIATE CHARACTERISTICS		
APPROACHES TO LEARNING		
KNOWLEDGE AND SKILLS		
INTERESTS AND CULTURAL HERITAGE		

REFLECTING ON IMPLEMENTATION

Did you teach the lesson as planned? What modification did you make either before or during implementation?

Were the processes/activities you developed effective in making the lesson student focused? What evidence supports your conclusions? What might you do differently the next time you use these processes/activities?

How effective were the products in demonstrating what your students learned? What evidence supports your conclusions? Did the products provide enough differentiation opportunities for students to demonstrate their understanding and/or skill? What might you do differently in designing similar products for future lessons?

NOTES

PART IV

THINKING ABOUT KNOWLEDGE OF STUDENTS AS IT APPLIES TO TEACHING

OBJECTIVES:

- USE GATHERED INFORMATION TO PLAN INSTRUCTION AND/OR ASSESSMENT STRATEGIES THAT ARE APPROPRIATE FOR THE TWO FOCUS STUDENTS.

- REFLECT ON THE NEXT STEPS YOU WANT TO TAKE TO GET TO KNOW A GREATER NUMBER OF YOUR STUDENTS ON A MORE MEANINGFUL LEVEL.

Today's educators agree that students learn in different ways and that their learning can be strongly influenced by their own individual talents, interests, family background, culture, socioeconomic situation, and prior experiences. Each is an individual, with his or her own personal history, ways of responding to and learning from the world, interests and passions, dreams and aspirations.

By now, you probably have a fuller understanding of how these differences might affect student learning, and how important it is to develop a deeper knowledge of these various aspects of your students—knowledge you will acquire through your own sensitive, systematic, and unbiased exploration of your students' individual personalities, backgrounds, abilities, interests, and learning needs and preferences. And you likely have at least a beginning understanding of some of the ways you can use knowledge to develop a more individualized, student-focused approach to instructional practices.

Finding out all you can about your students' individual differences will help you as you plan for, and implement, the best possible instruction for your students. You will be able to use this information to modify instruction so that it is at once challenging but accessible, so that learners come away with the important understandings and skills they need for future learning. For example, you can use this knowledge to plan instruction that will help struggling students focus on and master essential understandings and skills. At the same time, you can ensure that advanced learners spend their time grappling with challenging, more complex problems rather than spending time on what they already know.

In other words, you use this information to meet students where they are in each aspect of their learning—and then to help them move ahead. This knowledge of your students will help you make learning engaging, relevant, and accessible for your students. It

will help you determine specific ways to help each student learn as deeply and as quickly as possible. By applying this knowledge of your students carefully and thoughtfully, you will be able to adapt instruction appropriately, rather than haphazardly, to help move your students' learning to deeper levels.

As you become more accustomed to working with this student-focused approach, you will begin to see more opportunities to use your knowledge of your students to make learning more engaging. You may begin by adapting just one or two aspects of your practice, perhaps the content in a particular unit, the materials and resources your students might use, or one or two learning activities. Later, as you develop your knowledge of your students and expand your repertoire of strategies, you will use this approach in many more areas of your practice. At first, you may find it best to carefully plan each modification. With practice, however, you will eventually find it easier to use what you know about your students more spontaneously, when moments of opportunity present themselves.

This is not to say, however, that you must individualize every aspect of instruction. There are also times when lessons, materials, assessments, and the like should be consistent. Modify your instructional practices only when (1) you see a student need, or (2) you are convinced that modifying an approach will increase the likelihood that the student will gain deeper understanding or master important concepts or skills as a result.[40]

As you begin to incorporate a deeper knowledge of your students into your daily practice, also keep in mind the learning goals you have for your students as well as the essential concepts, principals, and skills you want them to acquire. By focusing on essentials, and then modifying your practices to accommodate the specific needs of your students, you will make their learning experience deeper, more exciting, and more purposeful.

BEFORE YOU BEGIN

Part IV of this minicourse is designed to guide you through a review of the process of collecting important information about your students, thinking about what this information means in terms of their learning and your instructional practice, and applying it to the strategies, lessons, or material with the intent of addressing a student need.

Before beginning, review each of the elements that comprise "Knowledge of Students" and what they entail. Think about their significance in the context of engaged learning, and how you might use new knowledge of your students to create a more engaging, flexible, student-focused learning atmosphere for your students.

---

[40] *Differentiated Classroom* (p. 11).

THE NEXT STEP

Now that you have a deeper knowledge of the four "Demonstrating Knowledge of Students" elements, the many investigative tools you can use to enhance your knowledge of the students you teach, and the many ways you can use what you learn about your students to improve your classroom practices, it is time to dive further into the Investigative Process for Building Knowledge of Students. As you know, this investigative process, as Figure 4.1 illustrates, is designed to help you gather the information you need to better know your students, using a purposeful, systematic, and efficient approach. The ultimate goal is twofold:

■ to support and enhance your knowledge of your students as it relates to teaching and learning, and

■ to advance your skill in the specific element(s) and tools you choose to explore.

The Investigative Process presented in this minicourse is designed to help you gather useful information about your students systematically, purposefully, and efficiently. It consists of five steps:

■ **Identify**

■ **Gather Information**

■ **Interpret Information**

■ **Apply New Understanding**

■ **Assess Progress and Plan Next Steps** (to determine starting points for your next cycle of investigation)

As you become more familiar with this process, you will see that it can (and should) be a dynamic and ongoing process. It should become integral to your practice, supporting and enhancing your efforts to give every student an equal opportunity to be successful in school.

While you work your way through this Investigative Process (which, to clarify, is focused on developing a deeper understanding of your students), you should also be reflecting on your own learning in the instructional skill known as "Knowledge of Students." The work you will be doing during this phase of the minicourse has twofold significance: (1) It will provide you with important information about your student(s), which you will use to address their learning needs; and (2) you will be deepening your own learning with respect to the skills and knowledge that relate to the component: Demonstrating Knowledge of Students.

This means that at the same time you are collecting evidence about your student(s), you should also be thinking about your own professional development: what represents professional growth in this instructional skill (your own personal goal for change), what constitutes evidence of that growth, and how will you be able to collect or demonstrate that evidence. As you proceed in the Investigative Process you will be collecting two types of evidence: (1) evidence that you will use to deepen your knowledge of your student(s) and (2) evidence of your own professional growth and effect on student learning.

THE INVESTIGATIVE PROCESS FOR BUILDING KNOWLEDGE OF STUDENTS

STEP 1: IDENTIFY

As you begin your investigation, identify

- Student(s) selected for investigation

- Your rationale, goal(s), and/or questions for the investigation

- Element(s) to be explored:

  — Characteristics of the age group

  — Students' varied approaches to learning

  — Students' skills and knowledge

  — Students' interests and cultural heritage

- Appropriate Investigative Tools

STEP 2: GATHER INFORMATION

Use selected Investigative Tools to collect information about identified

- Student(s)

- Element(s)

STEP 3: INTERPRET INFORMATION

Interpret the gathered information to determine students'

- Individual strengths and interests
- Cultural heritage
- Cognitive, emotional, and/or social development
- Learning styles

based on selected elements for investigation

STEP 4: APPLY NEW UNDERSTANDING

Apply the knowledge base to develop or revise approaches to effectively meet individual learning needs via

- Curriculum design
- Instructional planning and strategies
- Assessment methods

STEP 5: ASSESS PROGRESS AND PLAN NEXT STEPS

Collect and interpret evidence of student progress and plan for next steps.

Figure 4.1: The Five Steps of the Investigative Process

The Investigative Process for Building Knowledge of Students — A Review

Step 1: Identify

You begin by identifying a student (or group of students) for investigation (as you did at the end of Part I). This may be a student who is struggling with a concept or who seems capable of taking on more challenging work but for some reason isn't. It might be a student who, although clearly capable, tends to be disengaged from classroom activities, perhaps daydreaming, doodling, or chatting with a neighboring student.

At the same time you are identifying the students who will be the focus of your investigations, you need to decide *why* you are focusing on these students. That is, you need to clearly and explicitly identify your goal(s) and rationale(s) for the investigations, and/or any questions you wish to address. Now is a good time to revisit Activity 2.5 and the **Investigative Process** charts you completed for your two students selected for focus. Are there additional goals you want to add or modifications you want to make to the goals and rationales recorded? Are the "Questions to Answer" still appropriate? Are there additional questions to add and more information you want to collect?

The following section provides a review of the kinds of knowledge that are helpful to have about your students and how that knowledge can help your instructional practice.

1. **Understanding age-group characteristics** (intellectual, social, and emotional), also called "milestones" in some literature, will give you an idea about what to expect from students of different ages. Although it's normal for students to exhibit slight variations from the "norm," students who seem to be developing outside the expected range may be in need of extra attention. Recognizing these situations gives you a chance to identify such students, seek out explanations for these variations, and the information you need to plan instruction that accommodates their needs.

2. **Knowing about the ways students are best able to learn** — their learning styles and preferences and the obstacles that may get in the way of their learning, such as learning disabilities or language barriers — will provide you with useful information as you plan instructional assessment strategies. In addition, understanding how different specific environmental factors (light and noise levels, time of day, seating arrangements) can influence the way some students learn can help you modify your classroom to help students feel more comfortable or at ease. Similarly, knowing that

certain students are more engaged in the morning than later in the day gives you the information you need to plan your day.

3. **Identifying what students understand about subject areas and material that were previously taught** is essential for planning future teaching. It is also critical to know if students are holding on to any misunderstandings or misconceptions. These must be corrected. Students are able to best understand new information when they can attach it to accurate understandings of previously learned material.

4. **Knowing where students come from** — literally where they live, and figuratively what their families expect of them — can be helpful in understanding their expectations of themselves and of you, as well as their motivations. For example, children whose families have extremely rigid expectations of excellent grades in all subjects or those with little or no family support, limited resources, and few educated role models may be operating in very stressful home environments. It is essential for the teacher to know about these situations in order to better connect with students as learners.

5. **Understanding the influence and importance of cultural heritage in students' lives** is essential for providing them with successful learning opportunities. Understanding the link between culture and learning differences will tell you a lot about your students' learning preferences, the behaviors they are likely to value (independence vs. strong personal relationships with peers or teachers, for example), level of competitiveness, preference for learning broad concepts rather than distinct facts and specifics. However, although researchers have established certain commonalities among various cultures, they also agree that "within a group, variations are as great as commonalities" (Guild & Garger, 1998). For example, although researchers have established that culture affects one's approach to learning, they also agree that distinct learning-style patterns do not fit a specific cultural group.[41] Cultural expectations also vary among students, and the degree to which students adhere to these expectations and norms also varies. Teachers who increase their knowledge about how these expectations influence their students, and are sensitive to the individual variations within these groups, will more effectively connect with those students in the classroom. They can also use this knowledge and sensitivity to contribute to a classroom environment of acceptance and openness.

6. **Knowing what interests your students** provides you with many avenues through which you can teach concepts and skills — such as strategies that give students a chance to show their interests and knowledge using skills they have already acquired or with which they are comfortable.

---

[41] Guild & Garger. (1998). *Marching to Different Drummers*. ASCD: Alexandria, VA. (p. 31).

Finally, once you know what sort of information you need, you will be able to determine which Investigative Tools will be most useful at this stage of your investigation. Revisit Part II to refresh your memory regarding tools and models like Gardner's theory of Multiple Intelligences, Piaget's theory of Cognitive Development, "Kidwatching," and interest surveys.

STEP 2: GATHER INFORMATION

As you continue to use your Investigative Tools to gather information about your students, the following list can help you match the kinds of information you are seeking with the Investigative Tools that can help you find that information.

AGE-GROUP CHARACTERISTICS

The following resources can provide you with general information about age-group or grade-level expectations, to help you build your knowledge base.

- Current teacher-education publications that discuss the topic or focus on specific age groups or grade levels

- Up-to-date research reports (Try ERIC Digests, a searchable database of short reports on topics of prime current interest in education, designed to provide an overview of information on a given topic, plus references to items providing more detailed information: http://www.ed.gov/databases/ERIC_Digests/index/abtERICDig.html/)

- In-service workshops

- Discussions with colleagues (fellow teachers, guidance counselors)

- Discussions with child-development experts (teacher educators, psychologists, social workers)

- Your own experiences in the classroom over time, particularly through systematic and well-documented observation (including "kidwatching")

- Comparisons with other students

- Resources listed in Appendix B

VARIED APPROACHES TO LEARNING

The descriptions provided in Part II of this minicourse offer an overview of various theories on learning styles. Learning-style theory is a complex topic that requires thoughtful study. For that reason, it is suggested that you spend time becoming familiar with various theories through some of the resources listed in Appendix B. You might also consider investigating further on the Internet.

Once you feel comfortable with some of these concepts and their applications, you begin to gather information about the student or students in your investigation. Revisit Part II of this workbook to review the Investigative Tools and to continue to select the tools most useful for your current investigations based on the questions you want to answer about Students A and B.

SKILLS AND KNOWLEDGE

As you may already know, a teacher's understanding of her/his students' knowledge and skill levels is critical to planning and implementing effective instruction. As discussed in Part II, there are numerous means to assessing children's abilities and understanding. Such Investigative Tools include: pre- and post-testing; K-W-L-Q charts; "kidwatching;" student interviews; and academic games.

It is important to have and be able to easily access a repertoire of tools to provide students a variety of ways to show what they know and can do. Ascertaining students' current skill levels and subject-matter knowledge, along with comparing this information to your own expectations and age-appropriate standards, set the stage for instruction that meets the individual needs of every student.

> Ascertaining students' current skill levels and subject-matter knowledge, along with comparing this information to your own expectations and age-appropriate standards, set the stage for instruction that meets the individual needs of every student.

INTERESTS AND CULTURE

There are many ways to get to know the interests of your students, as well as their cultural backgrounds and values.

- **Conversing** with your students and their families, both formally and informally, can be very enlightening when you are getting to know the interests and values of your students. These conversations can shed light on deeply held family values, as well as the family's expectations of the student (this might include academic, professional, and behavioral expectations, to name a few). Using active listening skills will help you to clarify what you hear families saying about their expectations for their children and for you, their

> Using active listening skills will help you to clarify what you hear families saying about their expectations for their children and for you, their teacher.

teacher. Once you understand these expectations, you will have a better idea of how to approach learning with this student and the kinds of support you will receive from the student's home.

- **Interacting** with the people living in the community in which you teach is also a good way to observe and learn about the diverse cultures that make up your school community. Diverse cultures must be valued throughout the curriculum and among the members of the school community. Many communities sponsor cultural, art, social, and religious events that are open to the public. Attending these will give you a chance to absorb the various differences and commonalities among cultures and religious groups. Finding this common ground, and gaining a better understanding of the unique customs, traditions, and belief systems of these groups will help you to better understand how these affiliations influence your students. Students need to know that their cultural backgrounds are respected and understood, and your participation— where appropriate—shows that you value knowing about them.

- **Other adults** who interact with your students may be able to help you better understand student interests, as well as the family and cultural values that they see as influencing your students. These include, but are not limited to: other teachers, guidance counselors, coaches, as well as the adults who supervise or participate in sports, social or religious organizations, cultural organizations, after-school activities, and other nonacademic activities that encourage students to interact with different peer groups and adults.

- **Resources**, including research reports, academic publications, professional development publications, and the resources listed in Appendix B of this minicourse.

STEP 3: INTERPRET INFORMATION

Once you have collected as much relevant information as possible about the students you are focusing on for this investigation, you are ready to sort, analyze, and use the information to develop a deeper knowledge of the students with respect to the "Knowledge of Students" element(s) with which your investigation is concerned. You need to do this thoughtfully, without preconceived notions about these students or their backgrounds. Your goal is to use this information to help your modify your current practices in ways that will help these students achieve their full potential as learners.

It is important to keep in mind that interpreting information, even when based on evidence, is always dynamic and ever changing as new information and evidence are gathered.

More than likely, you will have a number of new insights about these students. Use the information you have gathered about these students to describe what you have learned. You may decide, after sifting through the information you have gathered, that you need to collect more information before you can move on to the next step — applying the information appropriately to advance the students' learning. It is important to keep in mind that interpreting information, even when based on evidence, is always dynamic and ever changing as new information and evidence are gathered.

STEP 4: APPLY NEW UNDERSTANDING

Now you need to apply what you now know about your students to your curriculum design, instructional planning, teaching strategies, and assessment methods.

In order to achieve your ultimate goal — to adjust your instructional practice in a way that will maximize student learning — you will need to work with these students as you *now* know them. You may not need to make changes in all aspects of your practice; indeed, it may be entirely inappropriate to do so. Depending on the situation and what you learn, your changes may be as simple as giving your students choices about which homework assignments to do, or as complex as modifying your instructional delivery to accommodate a range of learning styles, by including more visual representations of content or by designing specialized assessments for a student who displays a high degree of test anxiety.

> ### NOTE:
>
> It is impossible, as well as impractical, for teachers to accommodate every lesson to the learning needs of each and every student in the class. In fact, although it is important to accommodate students in ways that will advance their learning, it is equally as important to help students adapt to and become more comfortable in learning situations that are not particularly "ideal" for their particular learning style.

Below are some examples of areas of change you might want to pursue:

- Changes in **instructional** or **curricular choices** might mean altering how you present information to students, or redefining what constitutes critical information to be learned at the grade level or discipline you teach. Specifically, if a student is a visual learner and you find you *must* lecture, you might write notes on the chalkboard or on an overhead projector while you are talking so that visual learners can focus on the notes while they listen. In another case, you might rework a unit of study by including strategies for differentiating instruction, such as stations, choice boards, or agendas.

- Changes in **assessment offerings** might mean that you move to student-selected assessment modalities, where you give your students options that demonstrate learning but allow for student strengths to be used to illustrate new understandings. You might modify an existing assignment. For example, students who are not able to completely express what they know in an essay might be given the option of presenting their learning in an oral format.

- Changes in **teaching style** might mean that you match your teaching style to various learning styles. You can do this by employing several different modes of teaching a subject or topic, or by using many teaching styles within one lesson. You might also use learning groups more frequently, present students with more assignment options, and incorporate student interests and backgrounds into discussions and learning activities in ways that make the topics more relevant and meaningful for the students.

STEP 5: ASSESS PROGRESS AND PLAN NEXT STEPS

> *If you are convinced your students have indeed benefited from the changes or adaptations you have implemented, take time to evaluate exactly **how** they have benefited.*

After you have integrated your knowledge of students into your teaching, you will want to collect evidence or data for evaluating the success of your investigation and the effect your new knowledge has had on student learning. With as much objectivity as possible, analyze whether or not this new knowledge of your students (and your application of that knowledge to your practice) has benefited the students you chose for this investigation. If you are convinced your students have indeed benefited from the changes or adaptations you have implemented, take time to evaluate exactly *how* they have benefited. Also, try to determine what other steps would further this improvement. Use this evaluation to establish starting points for your next cycle of investigation.

This end-of-process assessment can also let you know if additional knowledge about one of these students would further benefit your instructional choices or the student's opportunities to learn.

This Investigative Process is ongoing and dynamic. Be prepared to reexamine your original goals and expectations, and to evaluate whether or not they are still appropriate—and to change those goals if they are not. You may find that you need to revise your goals or expectations for your students now that you better understand them. Don't be surprised if you find this new knowledge of your students changes some of the perceptions or expectations you have held about them.

This Investigative Process is ongoing and dynamic.

Example 1

For example, let's assume the goal set for a particular student is for him to begin to interact more with his peers. The teacher has developed a new understanding of the cultural expectations this student has grown up with, and this information explains the student's lack of peer interactions in class. Based on this information, the teacher understands that this student is probably comfortable with his apparent lack of peer interaction, even though it had originally appeared that the student was isolated and lonely. After investigation, the teacher finds that the student eats lunch with students who share similar cultural values and that he has extensive peer relationships within his cultural community outside of school. Clearly, the original goal of gaining a better understanding of the student has been achieved. However, a secondary goal of helping the student to develop closer peer relationships needs thoughtful, sensitive consideration. The teacher may decide to reshape the original goal, focusing on encouraging the student to learn to work and interact with students who do not share his cultural heritage or values. In the meantime, in physical education class, the teacher assigns the student to be coach of the day for the class game. Before the game, the teacher meets with the student to help him devise a plan for how he will convey strategies verbally with the team's members, as well as appropriate ways to praise team members when they demonstrate their skills and knowledge of the game.

Example 2

A new student joins the school and is placed in an eighth-grade math class. Because the student is misbehaving in class and refuses to do homework (but is always able to answer questions posed to the class), the teacher decides to get a better understanding of the student. The teacher begins an Investigative Process by first reviewing the student's earlier report cards and standardized test scores. The teacher also speaks with the school's guidance counselor, who had met with the student on several occasions. These resources indicate: (1) the student understands eighth-grade math concepts, (2) scored in the 90th percentile on standardized tests, and (3) was an "A" student in her previous school. The teacher interprets this information to mean that the student is not being challenged in the regular math class, and attributes the student's classroom misbehavior and lack of effort on homework as signs of boredom. In the teacher's opinion (based on a careful assessment of the evidence at hand), this evidence also explains why the student is able to answer all of the in-class questions. The teacher talks with the student, who confirms that she is bored in class and has already done most of the work the current class is now doing. She explains that her previous school had a different way of teaching math and, even though her report card said she had been in a regular math class during the previous year, she had also received tutoring to enrich her learning. The teacher and the student decide that, with her parent's approval, she should be moved to a higher-level math class, where she will be challenged. Once this change is made, the student's classroom behavior becomes appropriate, she completes her homework, and is actively involved in class learning activities.

Related Activities

Directions: The following activities move you through the remaining steps of the Investigative Process. You will need to go back to Part II Related Activities to complete the second section of the **Investigative Process** charts.

	COMPLETED
4.1 **Gathering evidence of your own learning.** Once you have completed the five steps of the Investigative Process, you need to gather evidence of your own performance in this skill, as well as evidence of an investigation's impact on student learning. It is important for you to take time to reflect on what changes in your classroom will provide evidence of your own growth. Use **My Minicourse Journal** to record your thoughts about assessing your own learning and proficiency.	
4.2 Up to this point in the minicourse, you have moved through the first two steps of the Investigative Process—Step 1: Identify and Step 2: Gather Information. You are now at the important steps of Interpret Information (Step 3) and Apply New Understanding (Step 4), as discussed in Part IV. It is important to organize and document each step in one location. To that end, you use **Investigative Process — Part 2** charts located in Part II Related Activities to record information for Steps 3 and 4.	

NOTE:

As you complete the **Investigative Process — Part 2** charts, it will be very important to continually reference the information you have already posted in the **Investigative Process — Part 1** charts, also located in Part II Related Activities.

a. **The Investigative Process — Step 3: Interpret Information.** Collected information will only be useful if it is carefully reviewed and interpreted. You should now begin this step, recording your understanding of what your collected information means under the column entitled "Interpretation." Keep in mind that interpretations are never absolute or final! As you continue to gather information about your students and build your knowledge base, your understanding of them will become more multi-dimensional and possibly quite different than your original understandings based on more simplistic interpretations.

b. **The Investigative Process — Step 4: Apply New Understanding.** Just as collected information becomes more useful when thoughtfully interpreted, interpretations become more useful when applied to one's practice — in this case, to specific teaching and assessment approaches to better understand and serve Students A and B. Step 4: Apply New Understanding is broken out into two parts: Implications for Instruction/Assessment; and Action to be Taken. At this time, you should be ready to begin completing these two columns located on the **Investigative Process — Part 2** charts. Refer to the sample chart located in Part II Related Activities as an example and a guide.

c. **The Investigative Process — Step 5: Assess Progress and Plan Next Steps.** Without completing this final step — assessing progress — the investigation's usefulness is minimal. By reviewing and reflecting on tangible evidence and observable outcomes, you can determine the effectiveness of

	COMPLETED
the investigation; assess your new understanding of the student(s), and the impact of the investigation on student learning. Identify evidence of learning and plans for next steps in the right-hand column of the **Investigative Process — Part 2** charts (return to Part II of this minicourse).	
4.3 As the final part of Step 5: Assess Progress, you are to write short narratives for Students A and B, assessing their progress and your plans for next steps. Use the space entitled **Investigative Process Narratives**, which follows, to record your narrative summaries. A sample is provided below. It relates to the scenario used for the sample **Investigative Process — Parts 1 and 2** charts located in Part II Related Activities.	

SAMPLE NARRATIVE

I was able to capitalize on Student A's interest in photography in order to increase his engagement in science. Rather than doodling in his notebook and staring out the window, Student A took an active role in completing lab assignments and working with peers. He was willing and eager to share his knowledge of and interest in photography and cameras with the class, both in whole-class and small-group venues. His ability to concentrate and focus is greatly increased when he is working with concrete materials that can be used to represent abstract concepts. His level of participation is higher when he is able to reference written directions that guide his participation. His interaction with peers is much improved when given a medium, such as photography, with which to communicate. As next steps, I plan to encourage him to continue to share his passion for photography with the class, such as becoming the "class photographer." For future lessons and science labs, I plan to make sure that there are always written directions for students to reference and concrete examples or applications of the often abstract concepts covered in science.

my minicourse
Journal

Take a moment to review the work you have completed, to date, on your two **Investigative Process** charts for Students A and B from the perspective of your own growth and learning.

1. *What evidence do you already have of your own learning about the component "Demonstrating Knowledge of Students"? Try to be as specific as you can.*

2. *As you prepare to interpret information and apply your new understanding to your practice, what types of evidence will you want to be aware of and gather about your own performance and growth as a teacher?*

Student A:

Student B:

PART V

OBJECTIVES:

- REFLECT ON AND SELF-ASSESS YOUR SUCCESS IN GATHERING INFORMATION ABOUT YOUR STUDENTS AND USING THAT INFORMATION TO PLAN ENGAGING LEARNING EXPERIENCES.

- CELEBRATE SUCCESS!

- PLAN NEXT STEPS FOR GROWTH IN GATHERING AND USING KNOWLEDGE OF STUDENTS.

YOUR CONTINUING PROGRESS

This minicourse has guided you through a relatively intense and comprehensive overview of a unique but essential element of good teaching: knowledge of students. Among other things, you have explored:

- what constitutes important, learning-related knowledge of students;

- how developing a deeper knowledge of students and applying that knowledge can make learning more engaging and therefore more effective;

- theories, models, and various other tools that are useful for developing deeper knowledge of students and their learning;

- some basic but essential teaching and assessment approaches that support and are enhanced by teachers' understanding of their students' interests, backgrounds, personalities, readiness levels, and various learning needs.

At the same time, you have learned a systematic approach for deepening your knowledge of your students and applying that knowledge in ways that support and encourage your students' learning efforts.

The cycle of learning is dynamic and ongoing, for teachers as well as for their students. As you look back at the steps you have taken to learn more about your students and to use that knowledge to more fully engage your students in learning, you should also be looking forward, toward the next steps you will take to improve your skill in these areas. The work you have done to deepen your knowledge of your students and using that knowledge to develop a more student-focused approach to teaching is an important step in the advancement of your teaching practice, and it also maps the way to possible future advancement.

In Part V of this minicourse, checklists prompt you to reflect on the successes and challenges you encountered while gathering information about your students and using that information to develop individualized, student-focused classroom strategies. Related Activities guide you in reflecting on what you learned through this effort, as well as in a constructive self-assessment of your performance. In charts that are provided, you document evidence of the kinds of changes you have made in your own practice that are directly related to the deeper knowledge you have of your students, and the effect those changes have had on the classroom environment. Finally, while this learning experience is still fresh in your mind, you take notes that may later help you set goals for your next incremental advancement.

As has been noted throughout this minicourse, students are wonderfully diverse, ever-growing, ever-changing individuals. Each possesses a unique way of learning, seeing, and experiencing the world and reacting to those experiences. These differences result from their own innate physical, mental, and emotional mechanisms, as well as their personal sets of life experiences. And every single one of these students — regardless of their abilities, talents, needs, age, culture, race, ethnicity, socioeconomic status, or gender — has a right to be given an equal opportunity to reach his or her full potential as a learner.

Developing a deeper knowledge of your students' backgrounds, personalities, abilities, skills, interests, and needs helps you examine your own instructional practices and become more sensitive to providing the diverse types of learning experiences that will help each of your students. The more you know about your students' individual learning needs, the better able you will be to provide learning opportunities and structures that are responsive to those needs. To provide effective, engaging instruction, you need to be able to accommodate and capitalize on your students' full range of exciting, sometimes challenging, gifts and needs.

> *Accepting your students as individuals and using that knowledge is one way you can help them reach for their metaphorical stars.*

Understanding and respecting who your students are, where they come from, and where they hope to go is a small but critical part of ensuring that every student is given the best chance possible to succeed in learning and in fulfilling his or her dreams. Accepting your students as individuals and using that knowledge is one way you can help them reach for their metaphorical stars.

Due to the wide-ranging and complex proficiencies upon which this area of classroom practice depends, it is important to remember that developing skill in these areas takes time and systematic effort. This minicourse encourages you to work toward increased proficiency one step at a time, and to allow yourself ample practice with the dynamic, ongoing process described. The first steps you take toward increasing your proficiency in this area may only emphasize the complexity of the process. This learning is critical to your advancement, so be sure to acknowledge and celebrate any progress you have made. Your appreciation of the complexity and importance of the task before you, your willingness to proceed even when progress is difficult or seems to exceed your grasp, and your ability to celebrate your own success will help you begin the cycle anew — refreshed, recharged, and eager to do what it takes to foster success among your students.

REFLECTING ON YOUR ACCOMPLISHMENTS

Part I of this minicourse introduced you to the level-of-performance scale associated with knowledge of students included in *Enhancing Professional Practice: A Framework for Teaching*. As you know, self-assessing *before* you undertake new learning as well as *after* is the most effective way to measure growth attributable to this new learning. While it is not critical that you use this level-of-performance scale to assess your progress in mastering this new knowledge, it is important that you identify the progress you have made and that you look to your students for evidence of your increased proficiency. This minicourse has focused on the importance of developing and demonstrating knowledge of students. This knowledge has been defined as:

> As you know, self-assessing *before* you undertake new learning as well as *after* is the most effective way to measure growth attributable to this new learning.

- Knowledge of Characteristics of Age Group

- Knowledge of Students' Varied Approaches to Learning

- Knowledge of Students' Skills and Knowledge

- Knowledge of Students' Interests and Cultural Heritage

While you have primarily focused on two students as you've completed work during this minicourse, it is important to widen the lens and see how your growing knowledge of students is impacting your practice. The checklists on the following pages provide questions that are intended to help you reflect on your practice in light of the elements that influence proficiency in knowledge of students. Depending on your level of proficiency prior to beginning this minicourse, some questions may not apply to you yet. As you consider each checkpoint, try to recall specific evidence of student success (such as student behaviors you observed, work samples, specific examples of student responses) to help you evaluate your own success with each element.

MAKING A CONNECTION

CHECKPOINTS

1. Recall the changes you have been making to your classroom practice as you have been developing your knowledge of students.

2. For each checkpoint in the four lists that follow, consider whether or not you have evidence that the checkpoint has been achieved (e.g., examples of student behavior, actual student responses, sample work).

3. In the box to the left of each checkpoint, place a checkmark to indicate that you have evidence of success in this area, or leave it blank to indicate that you do not yet have such evidence of success. List critical pieces of evidence that support your conclusion.

KNOWLEDGE OF CHARACTERISTICS OF AGE GROUP

☐ Is the content of my lessons appropriate for the age and grade level of the student(s)? That is, do they take into account the students' developmental and age-related learning needs, knowledge, aptitudes, skills, interests, aspirations, and socialization?

Evidence:

☐ Are the learning activities associated with my lessons appropriate for the age and grade level of the student(s)?

Evidence:

☐ Are the instructional materials I used appropriate for the age and grade level of the student(s)?

Evidence:

☐ Is the classroom environment inviting and comfortable for students of this age or grade level?

Evidence:

☐ Do I structure and pace my lessons and associated activities appropriately for students of this age or grade level?

Evidence:

☐ Are assessment strategies appropriate for students of this age or grade level?

Evidence:

☐ Is the content of my lessons appropriate for this age or grade level?

Evidence:

☐ Are the activities associated with lessons appropriate for this age or grade level?

Evidence:

☐ Are the products and demonstrations that have resulted from these activities and assignments appropriate for this age or grade level?

Evidence:

☐ Is the content of lessons presented in a way that supports the learning needs and styles of the student(s)?

Evidence:

☐ Are learning activities provided that support the learning needs and styles of the student(s)?

Evidence:

☐ Do the learning activities and assignments invite students to apply their individual learning styles?

Evidence:

☐ Do lessons or learning activities give the student(s) a chance to expand their repertoire of preferred approaches to learning?

Evidence:

☐ Are the instructional materials available that support the learning needs and styles of the student(s)?

Evidence:

☐ Are assessment strategy options available that support the learning needs and styles of the student(s)?

Evidence:

☐ Is the classroom environment inviting and comfortable for the student(s) — does it support the learning needs and styles of the student(s)?

Evidence:

☐ Do learning and processing opportunities support the learning needs and styles of the student(s)?

Evidence:

☐ Do I observe signs of my students' intellectual engagement as they complete the activities and assignments?

Evidence:

☐ Do the products and demonstrations that have resulted from these activities provide opportunities for my students to best show the learning and/or skills they have achieved?

Evidence:

KNOWLEDGE OF STUDENTS' SKILLS AND KNOWLEDGE

☐ Does new content reflect students' prior learning, skills, and readiness levels?

Evidence:

☐ Does new content interest, challenge, and engage the student(s)?

Evidence:

☐ Is the new content at an appropriate level of difficulty — that is, is it challenging, but not so challenging that it intimidates or frustrates the student(s)?

Evidence:

☐ Are lessons, questions, and learning material respectful of and sensitive to the students' individual abilities?

Evidence:

☐ Do the learning activities and assignments invite students to apply their individual skills and abilities?

Evidence:

☐ Do the products and demonstrations that have resulted from these activities and assignments show that my students achieved the learning and/or skills I intended?

Evidence:

KNOWLEDGE OF STUDENTS' INTERESTS AND CULTURAL HERITAGE

☐ Are my students able to relate to and/or see the relevance of learning the new content?

Evidence:

☐ Do the learning activities and assignments invite students to apply their individual interests?

Evidence:

☐ Do my students find their activities and assignments interesting, challenging, and engaging?

Evidence:

☐ Do the lessons, activities, and assignments invite my students to bring their cultural backgrounds, individual experiences, and personal interests to bear on their learning?

Evidence:

☐ Have I completed and implemented any professional reading related to culturally responsive teaching and/or does my instruction incorporate a broad range of ethnic and cultural groups?

Evidence:

☐ Are lessons, questions, and learning material respectful of and sensitive to students' personal circumstances and cultural heritage?

Evidence:

☐ Are lessons, questions, and learning material respectful of and sensitive to students' individual abilities and backgrounds?

Evidence:

SELF-ASSESSING YOUR CURRENT PROFICIENCY

Now that you have completed this minicourse, take some time to assess your current knowledge of the students in your classroom and your ability to use that knowledge to advance their learning. The scale on the following page (Figure 5.1) describes four performance levels for demonstrating understanding of students and how that knowledge can be applied to instruction and assessment. You can use this scale to measure your progress in these areas and to identify areas on which you need to work.

As noted in Part I of this minicourse, the "unsatisfactory" level describes performance that demonstrates little or no knowledge of students' age-group expectations, backgrounds, skills, or interests, nor knowledge of why that information would be valuable to instruction and student learning. The "basic" performance level indicates a partial knowledge of students' age-group expectations, backgrounds, skills, and interests, and an attempt to use that knowledge in planning instruction for the class as a whole. The "proficient" level represents a solid, thorough knowledge of students' age-group expectations, backgrounds, skills, and interests, and clear evidence of its application to instructional and assessment strategies for groups of students. And the "distinguished" level describes thorough knowledge of students' age-group expectations, backgrounds, skills, and interests, and the ability to apply that knowledge when planning for individual student learning and assessment.

Remember that level-of-performance scales momentarily isolate an aspect of teaching practice in order to give one an opportunity to reflect upon that aspect and assess one's strengths or needs for growth. Your performance may change over time, depending on the teaching situation you find yourself in and the students you are working with. Clearly, your own professional development will also influence future performance. However, teachers who achieve a proficient level of skill in any given domain understand that, during daily practice, all components are interdependent and interwoven.

ELEMENT	LEVEL OF PERFORMANCE			
	UNSATISFACTORY	BASIC	PROFICIENT	DISTINGUISHED
KNOWLEDGE OF CHARACTERISTICS OF AGE GROUP	Teacher displays minimal knowledge of developmental characteristics of age group.	Teacher displays generally accurate knowledge of developmental characteristics of age group.	Teacher displays thorough understanding of typical developmental characteristics of age group as well as exceptions to general patterns.	Teacher displays knowledge of typical developmental characteristics of age group, exceptions to the patterns, and the extent to which each student follows patterns.
KNOWLEDGE OF STUDENTS' VARIED APPROACHES TO LEARNING	Teacher is unfamiliar with the different approaches to learning that students exhibit.	Teacher displays general understanding of the different approaches to learning that students exhibit.	Teacher displays solid understanding of the different approaches to learning that different students exhibit.	Teacher uses, where appropriate, knowledge of students' varied approaches to learning in instructional planning.
KNOWLEDGE OF STUDENTS' SKILLS AND KNOWLEDGE	Teacher displays little knowledge of students' skills and knowledge and does not indicate that such knowledge is valuable.	Teacher recognizes the value of understanding students' skills and knowledge but displays this knowledge for the class only as a whole.	Teacher displays knowledge of students' skills and knowledge for groups of students and recognizes the value of this knowledge.	Teacher displays knowledge of students' skills and knowledge for each student, including those with special needs.
KNOWLEDGE OF STUDENTS' INTERESTS AND CULTURAL HERITAGE	Teacher displays little knowledge of students' interests and cultural heritage and does not indicate that such knowledge is valuable.	Teacher recognizes the value of understanding students' interests and cultural heritage but displays this knowledge for the class only as a whole.	Teacher displays knowledge of the interests and cultural heritage of groups of students and recognizes the value of this knowledge.	Teacher displays knowledge of the interests and cultural heritage of each student.

Figure 5.1: A Level-of-Performance Scale for Demonstrating Knowledge of Students (from *Enhancing Professional Practice: A Framework for Teaching* by Charlotte Danielson).

Planning Future Advancement

The final step before repeating the learning cycle outlined in this minicourse is to use your self-assessment to begin planning the next steps of your professional development in this area. Take time to reflect on what you have learned, both in terms of the variety of approaches available to developing a deeper knowledge of students and their learning as well as your ability to use that knowledge to collect, interpret, and apply important new knowledge of students to your practice in ways that make learning more accessible for your students. Think, too, about the specifics of what you have learned in regard to the students in your classroom during this process. You will likely feel satisfied with certain areas of growth and practice. At the same time, you will probably see areas in which you could strengthen your skills. By taking notes and outlining plans now, you can begin devising a map to guide your future professional growth.

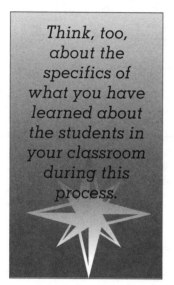

Think, too, about the specifics of what you have learned about the students in your classroom during this process.

For instance, your self-reflection may lead you to find that you are not as competent as you would like to be in understanding and using certain methods for gathering information about students' learning styles, interests, or cultural heritage. Or you may feel you need to think more deeply about how to interpret the information you collect so that you can use it to make meaningful changes in your practice. Or you may need to develop your skill in applying knowledge to develop a more student-focused approach to instruction. Perhaps you already know what new area(s) of knowledge of students you wish to explore, or you may have decided you would like to further explore the areas you have already been working with. Perhaps the changes you implemented as a result of what you have learned about your students didn't go far enough. Related Activities at the end of Part V guide your planning for future growth.

Later, when you repeat the learning cycle, you can review your notes before setting a new goal for your professional advancement. When that time arrives, you may follow your map exactly, or you may chart unanticipated territories. It matters not. The process of continually reflecting on and assessing your progress will pave your way to enhanced professional practice and improved student learning.

The PATHWISE Minicourse Learning Cycle

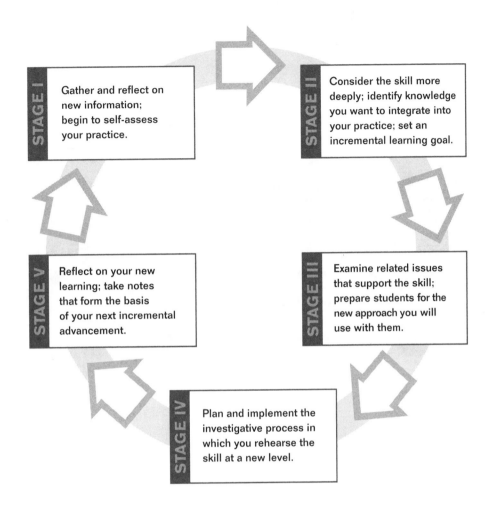

STAGE I
Gather and reflect on new information; begin to self-assess your practice.

STAGE II
Consider the skill more deeply; identify knowledge you want to integrate into your practice; set an incremental learning goal.

STAGE III
Examine related issues that support the skill; prepare students for the new approach you will use with them.

STAGE IV
Plan and implement the investigative process in which you rehearse the skill at a new level.

STAGE V
Reflect on your new learning; take notes that form the basis of your next incremental advancement.

As is the case with the PATHWISE minicourse cycle, the Investigative Process for developing deeper, more substantive knowledge of your students is both dynamic and ongoing. After reflecting on what you have learned about the students in your investigation, and self-assessing your success in applying that knowledge to enhance their learning, you will be ready to start anew—either to further understand how to help the students in your original investigation or to help other students in your classroom.

But the investment you make in this process is well worth the time and effort, since a thorough understanding of even a single element of one student's life or greater understanding of a variety of students will increase your effectiveness with teaching all your students.

Directions: The following activities are intended to help you self-assess your implementation of the Investigative Process completed during this minicourse as well as your current level of proficiency with the component, "Demonstrating Knowledge of Students." In addition, you are now ready to plan your next steps for professional growth as it relates to this component. The activities should be completed sequentially and in a manner that is conducive to your individual learning style.

	COMPLETED
5.1 Using **My Minicourse Journal**, which follows, reflect on your current knowledge of your students and how you now apply that knowledge to instruction and assessment.	
5.2 In the space entitled **My Next Steps**, which follows, jot down any and all aspects of your practice that you wish to refine in the future—either in your next learning cycle or later. Then, take some time to sort your long-term professional development goals from your next steps. Also, consider the scope of your plans and how you can achieve them incrementally. When you are ready to repeat the activities provided in this minicourse and as you plan new student investigations, remember to consider the notes you drafted in **My Next Steps.**	

my minicourse
Journal

1. INSTRUCTIONAL STRATEGIES

After developing a deeper, more substantive knowledge of your students, and learning about the many instructional strategies that can be used in your classroom to support their various learning needs, your instructional methods have probably changed.

a. Reflect on how your new knowledge of your students has influenced your instructional strategies. Using the chart below, list the changes you have made or plan to make in the way you teach particular topics or units. An example has been provided.

TOPIC/UNIT/LEARNING STANDARD	CHANGES IN INSTRUCTIONAL STRATEGIES
Example: Poetry Unit	• Used small groups for peer editing or feedback on original poems, rather than having students hand all poems to me in all draft states. • Used famous poems as models of various styles of poetry, rather than giving notes defining poetic styles. • Differentiated instruction using an "orbital studies" approach.

b. Give a detailed example of an adjustment you have made in an instructional strategy. Be as specific as possible and include the reasons for your change. This will force you to think through your rationales for change and see your own growth. For example:

In the past, it may have been your practice to assign students a chapter to read at home in preparation for a new unit, but you found that your students were not prepared for a class discussion when you began to teach the unit. To address this problem, you may have changed your strategy and instead asked students to read portions of a textbook aloud in class, and allowed time for questions and comments. Or you may have used a class discussion technique to get them interested in the topic. This change of approach ensured that your students had a common — and accurate — understanding of the topic before you began teaching it and, as a result, they were ready to learn new information in a more age-appropriate way.

Your own example:

2. Assessment Strategies

a. Use the chart that follows to document how you have modified or plan to modify your assessment strategies based on your new knowledge of your students. An example has been provided.

Topic/Unit/Learning Standard	Changes in Assessment Strategies
Example: Poetry Unit	• Created a "Coffee House" as the way to assess understanding of poetic styles, verbal skills, and listening skills, and to create an authentic environment for sharing original poems rather than having students merely hand in original poetry books for me to read and grade. • Required that students self-assess their own understanding and presentation using a rubric designed with student input rather than grading all of the poetry projects on an A-F scale. • Differentiated culminating project/product by giving students several options for demonstrating their knowledge/skill, including creating poetry books, setting original poems to music, or dramatizing poems.

b. Give a detailed example of an adjustment you have made in an assessment strategy. Be as specific as possible and include the reasons for your change. For example:

In the past, you may have had students complete a research paper to demonstrate their ability to interpret research, write a thesis statement, and organize information in a way that helps others understand it. In response to what you have learned about your students' individuality, you may have adjusted your strategy so that you can now assess those same skills by letting the students choose their own research assignments. Or you may now conference with each student about the topic and then craft individual contracts that include mutually agreed upon expectations that meet your criteria and give the students choice and input about how they will demonstrate their learning.

Your own example:

3. Planning Future Learning

This minicourse provided you with an overview of learning styles, ways of differentiating instruction, and information about different types of assessment strategies. In order to gain a more in-depth understanding of any or all of these topics, future learning may need to take place. Have you begun to delve into any of these areas? If so which ones and what have you learned that has been helpful in understanding your students? If not, which would you like to know more about?

4. Classroom Environment

a. What changes have you made in your classroom to address learning needs or the preferences of your students? Specifically, how do you think these changes helped these students?

b. What evidence do you have that your increased knowledge of your students has created positive change in your classroom? For example:

"Students compliment other students for age-appropriate classroom behavior" (e.g., "You did a great job organizing the books in our class library.") is evidence that students are supportive of one another. If this behavior is new and patterned after your own, then it is likely that your increased understanding of your students' age-appropriate behaviors is triggering change in your classroom. List as many observable examples of change as you can.

c. How has your increased knowledge of your students' age-appropriate behaviors and abilities, their learning styles, their academic and cultural backgrounds, and their interests helped you to create a learning environment in which students are more able to engage in the learning at hand? In what ways are they showing signs of being more engaged in learning? Describe the evidence of that engagement.

MY NEXT STEPS

This minicourse has provided you with an overview of learning styles, ways of differentiating instruction and assessment, and a process by which you can conduct your own investigations to learn more about your students in order to tailor your teaching to meet their individual needs. In order to gain a more in-depth understanding of any or all of these aspects of teaching, future study and learning should take place. **How do you plan to continue your learning as it relates to knowledge of students and to sharpen your investigative skills? After you have listed the ways you want to refine your practice, note which you see as short-term professional goals and which as long-term.** Use these notes as you plan your next incremental steps.

Appendix A
A Framework for Teaching

Domain 1	Domain 2
PLANNING AND PREPARATION	**THE CLASSROOM ENVIRONMENT**

Domain 1 — PLANNING AND PREPARATION

1a: Demonstrating Knowledge of Content and Pedagogy

Knowledge of content
Knowledge of prerequisite relationships
Knowledge of content-related pedagogy

1b: Demonstrating Knowledge of Students

Knowledge of characteristics of age group
Knowledge of students' varied approaches
to learning
Knowledge of students' skills and knowledge
Knowledge of students' interests and
cultural heritage

1c: Selecting Instructional Goals

Value
Clarity
Suitability for diverse students
Balance

1d: Demonstrating Knowledge of Resources

Resources for teaching
Resources for students

1e: Designing Coherent Instruction

Learning activities
Instructional materials and resources
Instructional groups
Lesson and unit structure

1f: Assessing Student Learning

Congruence with instructional goals
Criteria and standards
Use for planning

Domain 2 — THE CLASSROOM ENVIRONMENT

2a: Creating an Environment of Respect and Rapport

Teacher interaction with students
Student interaction

2b: Establishing a Culture for Learning

Importance of content
Student pride in work
Expectations for learning and achievement

2c: Managing Classroom Procedures

Management of instructional groups
Management of transitions
Management of materials and supplies
Performance of noninstructional duties
Supervision of volunteers and paraprofessionals

2d: Managing Student Behavior

Expectations
Monitoring of student behavior
Response to student misbehavior

2e: Organizing Physical Space

Safety and arrangement of furniture
Accessibility to learning and use of
physical resources

Figure A1. Components of Professional Practice

Domain 3
INSTRUCTION

3a: Communicating Clearly and Accurately

Directions and procedures
Oral and written language

3b: Using Questioning and Discussion Techniques

Quality of questions
Discussion techniques
Student participation

3c: Engaging Students in Learning

Representation of content
Activities and assignments
Grouping of students
Instructional materials and resources
Structure and pacing

3d: Providing Feedback to Students

Quality: accurate, substantive, constructive, and specific
Timeliness

3e: Demonstrating Flexibility and Responsivenes

Lesson adjustment
Response to students
Persistence

Domain 4
PROFESSIONAL RESPONSIBILITIES

4a: Reflecting on Teaching

Accuracy
Use in future teaching

4b: Maintaining Accurate Records

Student completion of assignments
Student progress in learning
Noninstructional records

4c: Communicating with Families

Information about the instructional program
Information about individual students
Engagement of families in the instructional program

4d: Contributing to the School and District

Relationships with colleagues
Service to the school
Participation in school and district projects

4e: Growing and Developing Professionally

Enhancement of content knowledge and pedagogical skill
Service to the profession

4f: Showing Professionalism

Service to students
Advocacy
Decision making

Figure A1. Components of Professional Practice

Appendix B: Resources

General

Atwell, N. (1987). *In the middle: Writing, reading, and learning with adolescents.* Portsmouth, NH: Boynton/Cook Publishers, Inc.

A "how-to" book filled with examples of how knowing students can be used to teaching language arts in middle school.

Danielson, C. (1996). *Enhancing professional practice: A framework for teaching.* Alexandria, VA: ASCD.

Funderstanding.com. *Engaging kids.* Available: www.funderstanding.com/engaging_kids.cfm

Jensem. E. *Teaching with the brain in mind.* Alexandria, VA: ASCD.

Maryland State Department of Education. (n.d.). School Improvement in Maryland: Teaching and Assessing Content Standards. Available: www.mdk12.org/practices.

Very user-friendly site that covers many topics that have that has to do with good teaching and successful learning. Topics cover everything from how children learn, to best teaching practices, and includes discussions of what has been learned from brain research, constructivism, multiple intelligences, and standards-based education—just to name a few.

Meece, J., & McColsky, W. (1997). *Improving student motivation: A guide for teachers and school improvement teams.* Tallahassee: FL: Southeast Regional Vision for Education.

Provides a general overview of research on student motivation in classroom and school settings, and a guide to help teachers and school teams to analyze the sources of students' motivational problems and consider changes that will improve motivation.

Ogle, D. M. (1986). K–W–L: A teaching model that develops active reading of expository text. *The Reading Teacher, 39*(6), 564-570.

Tileston, D. (2000). *10 best teaching practices: How brain research, learning styles, and standards define teaching competencies.* Thousand Oaks, CA: Corwin Press, Inc.

Age-group Characteristics

National Network for Child Care. Available: www.nncc.org/Child.Dev/child.dev.page.html

Wood, Chip. (1994). *Yardsticks: Children in the classroom, ages 4-14—A resource for parents and teachers.* Northeast Foundation for Children: Greenfield, MA.

A comprehensive, user-friendly guide offering concise descriptions of children's development. Includes charts summarizing growth patterns: physical, social, language, and cognitive; suggestions for curricular areas: reading, writing, mathematics, and thematic units; favorite books for different ages.

4MAT

McCarthy, B. (1987). *The 4MAT system: Teaching to learning styles with right/left mode techniques.* Barrington, IL: Excel.

McCarthy's 4MAT system. Includes a variety of sample lessons.

McCarthy, B. (1997). *About learning.* Barrington, IL: Excel.

Explains learning differences, focusing on McCarthy's 4MAT system.

Samples, B., Hammond, B., & McCarthy, B. (1980). *4MAT and science: Toward wholeness in science education.* Barrington, IL: Excel.

Illustrates how the 4MAT applies to the teaching of science; includes lesson plans.

See also Guild and Garger (1998).

APPROACHES TO LEARNING

Armstrong, Thomas. (1994). *Multiple intelligences in the classroom.* Association for Supervision and Curriculum Development.

A reader-friendly discussion of Gardner's theory of multiple intelligences and its application to teaching.

Goleman, D. (1995). *Emotional intelligence: why it can matter more than IQ.* New York: Bantam.

Describes emotional intelligence and its implications, including for learning. Argues that human competencies like self-awareness, self-discipline, persistence, and empathy are of greater consequence than IQ in much of life, and that children can—and should—be taught these abilities. Because emotional intelligence is not fixed at birth, Goleman outlines how adults as well as parents of young children can sow the seeds of emotional development.

Guild, P.B. and Garger, S. (1998). *Marching to different drummers, 2nd edition.* Alexandria, VA: Association for Supervision and Curriculum Development.

A reader-friendly discussion of learning styles and their application. Also includes extensive and thoughtful discussions on the importance of understanding student culture, learning styles in light of recent discoveries about the functioning of the brain, and how learning styles relate to Howard Gardener's theory of multiple intelligences.

ASSESSMENT

Center for Support of Teaching and Learning at Syracuse University. (n.d.). *Topics for teachers: Classroom assessment.* Available: http://cstl.syr.edu/cstl/t-l/cls_asmt.htm

Educational Testing Service. (1999). Letting students shine: Assessment to promote students in learning. *Focus 31.* Princeton, NJ: ETS. Available: comser@ets.org

Educational Testing Service. (2001). PATHWISE® Online: Fundamentals of Classroom Assessment.

Convenient, cost-effective, research-based course developed by the Teaching and Learning Division of ETS. Available for educators of elementary, upper elementary and middle school, and secondary school students. For information or to register, call 800-297-9051 or visit the Teaching and Learning Web site: www.ets.org/teachingandlearning.

Salend, Spencer J. (November 1995). Modifying tests for diverse learners. *Intervention in school and clinic,* 31(2), 84-90.

CONSTRUCTIVISM

Brooks, J. & Brooks, M.(1999). *In Search of understanding: The case for constructivist classrooms.* ASCD: Alexandria, VA.

Bruner, J. (1996). *The culture of education.* Cambridge, MA: Harvard University Press.

Bruner, J. (1960). *The process of education.* Cambridge, MA: Harvard University Press.

Outlines his constructivist theory of learning. Also proposes a "spiral curriculum."

Cooperative Learning

Dumas, A. (n.d.). *Cooperative learning response to diversity: All for one, one for all.* Available: www.cde.ca.gov/iasa/cooplrng2.html

Holubec, E., Johnson, D., & Johnson, R. (1994). *The new circles of learning: Cooperation in the classroom and school.* ASCD: Alexandria, VA.

Reinforces and expands cooperative learning practices found in *Circles of Learning: Cooperation in the Classroom*, to include the school and district. With thorough descriptions of cooperative learning and its supporting research, the authors explain why cooperation must strengthen schooling at every level. (Spanish-language edition also available.)

Cultural Heritage

Guild, P. (May 1994). The culture/learning style connection. *Educational Leadership*, 51(8). Available: www.ascd.org/readingroom/edlead/9405/guild.html

Differentiated Learning

Association for Supervision and Curriculum Development. *Differentiating instruction.* ASCD Web site: ascd.org/pdi/demo/diffinstr/differentiated1.html

Discusses differentiated instruction. Page links to other pages with examples from a high school and elementary school, key characteristics of a differentiated classroom, benefits, related readings, discussion, and related links to explore.

Hess, M.A. (March 26, 1999). *Teaching in mixed-ability classrooms: Teachers guide students down many paths to a common destination.* Wisconsin Education Association Council. Available: www.weac.org/kids/1998-99/march99/differ.htm

Holloway, J.H., (2000). Preparing Teachers for Differentiated Instruction. *Educational Leadership*, 58(1). Available: http://web.uvic.ca/~jdurkin/edd401su/Differentiated.html

This site is from an education course by Dr. John Durkin. It includes a diagram with suggestions for approaches to differentiated instruction. It also includes a listing of what differentiated instruction is and is not, rules of thumb on how to instruct, and management strategies.

Theroux, P. (2001). *Enhance learning with technology: Differential instruction.* Available: www.cssd.ab.ca/tech/oth/learn/differentiating.htm

Author provides a thorough site on differential instruction for a Canadian school district. Provides links to teacher attitudes, learning strategies, teacher resources, integrating technology, integrating outcomes, exploring projects, sample lesson plans, planning projects, thinking skills, developing Web pages, assessing, and tutorials.

Tomlinson, C.A., (1995). Differentiating instruction for advanced learners in the mixed-ability middle school classroom. (ERIC Document Reproduction Service No. E536) Available: www.ed.gov/databases/ERIC_Digests/ed389141.html

The ability to differentiate instruction for middle school aged learners is a challenge. Responding to diverse student needs found in inclusive, mixed-ability classrooms is particularly difficult. This digest provides an overview of some key principles for differentiating instruction, with an emphasis on the learning needs of academically advanced students.

Tomlinson, C.A. (1999). *The differentiated classroom: Responding to the needs of all learners.* ASCD: Alexandria, VA.

Tomlinson, C.A. (September 1999). Mapping a route toward differentiated instruction. *Educational Leadership,* 57(1). Available: www.ascd.org/pdi/demo/diffinstr/tomlinson2.html

Tomlinson, C.A., (2000). Differentiation of instruction in the elementary grades. (ERIC Document Reproduction Service NO. ED443572) Available: http://ericir.syr.edu/plweb-cgi/obtain.pl

Describes differentiated instruction, discusses the reasons for differentiated instruction and what makes it successful, and suggests how teachers may begin implementation.

Tomlinson, C.A., & Allan, S. D., (2000). Leadership for differentiating schools and classrooms. Available: www.ascd.org/readingroom/books/tonlinson00book.html

Two chapters from Tomlinson's publication: *Leadership for differentiating schools and classrooms,* published by the Association for Supervision and Curriculum Development. This book is designed for those in leadership positions to learn about differentiated instruction.

Willis, S., & Mann, L., (winter 2000). Differentiating instruction: Finding manageable ways to meet individual needs (excerpt). *Curriculum Update*. Available: www.ascd.org/readingroom/cupdate/200/1win.html

Based on the concept that "one size does not fit all," the authors describe the teaching philosophy of differentiated instruction. More teachers are determined to reach all learners, to challenge students who may be identified as gifted as well as students who lag behind grade level. This article excerpt describes the essential components of differentiated instruction beginning with three aspects of curriculum: content, process, and product.

Wehrmann, K.S. (September 2000). Baby steps, a beginner's guide: The journey to a differentiated classroom starts with small steps. *Educational Leadership*, 58(1). Available: www.ascd.org/readingroom/edlead/0009/wehrmann.html.

Provides useful suggestions about applying knowledge of students by differentiating the classroom.

DUNN AND DUNN

Carbo, M., Dunn, R., & Dunn, K. (1986). *Teaching students to read through their individual learning styles*. Englewood Cliffs, NJ: Prentice-Hall.

Dunn, R. (1983). Learning style & its relation to exceptionality at both ends of the spectrum. *Exceptional Children*, 4(6), 496-506.

Dunn, R., Beaudry, J. & Klavas, A. (1989). *Survey of research on learning styles. Educational Leadership*. 50-58.

Dunn, R. & Dunn, K. (1992). *Teaching secondary students through their individual learning styles: Practical approaches for grades 7-12*. Boston: Allyn and Bacon.

Dunn, R., Dunn, K., & Price, G.E. (1985). *Learning styles inventory (LSI): An inventory for the identification of how individuals in grades 3 through 12 prefer to learn*. Lawrence, KS: Price Systems.

The North Carolina Distance Education Partnership in Special Education. The Dunn and Dunn Learning Style Model of Instruction, Available: www.unc.edu/depts/ncpts/publications/learnstyles.htm

Learning Styles, Multiple Intelligences, Approaches to Learning

Armstrong, T. (1994). *Multiple intelligences in the classroom*. Alexandria, VA:ASCD.

Reader-friendly explanation of Gardner's theory of multiple intelligences and its proven application in school and the classroom. The book includes information on how to explore your own and your students' multiple intelligences, develop MI lessons, and conduct MI assessments.

Gardner, H. 1999. *The disciplined mind: what all students should understand*. New York: Simon and Schuster.

Gardner applies his own theories of multiple intelligences to current styles of teaching and determining what to teach. He recommends depth rather than coverage when teaching about a topic, and provides examples.

Golay, K. (1982). *Learning patterns and temperament styles*. Newport Beach, CA: Manas Systems.

Profiles four types of learners and offers specific suggestions for accommodating styles through tasks, subject interests, classroom climate, and physical environment.

Guild, P. & Garger, S. (1998). *Marching to different drummers* (2nd edition). Alexandria, VA: ASCD

Includes discussions on the importance of understanding student culture, learning styles in light of recent discoveries about the functioning of the brain, and how learning styles relate to Howard Gardner's theory of multiple intelligences.

Lawrence, G. (1982, 1993). *People types and tiger stripes, A practical guide to learning styles*. Gainsville, FL: Center for Applications of Psychological Type, Inc.

Gives overview of learning styles and offers practical suggestions for instruction, meeting students' developmental needs, and other educational applications.

O'Conner, T. (n.d.). *Using learning styles to adapt technology for higher education*. Center for Teaching and Learning, Indiana State University. Available: www.htctu.fhda.edu/prestools/ls/learning.html

Simon, A. & Byram, C. (1977). *You've got to reach 'em to teach 'em*. Dallas, TX: Training Associates Press.

Gives an overview of learning styles and their implications for teaching and learning. Offers many practical suggestions for teachers.

Keirsey, D. & Bates, M. (1978). *Please understand me, character and temperament types*. Del Mar, CA: Prometheus, Nemesis.

Offers introduction to personality typing based on the Myers-Briggs personality test — with a Jungian accent. Includes the 70-question "Keirsey Temperament Sorter," a sort of mini-Myers-Briggs test that places people in 1 of 16 personality types. Also presents four easy-to-remember temperament types — Dionysian (freedom first), Epimethean (wants to be useful), Promethean (desires power), and Apollonian (searches for self) — that underlie the 16 possible personalities identified by the test. The book then delves into a detailed analysis of each type, and offers general examples of each type in everyday life as well as in teaching and learning.

Keirsey, D. (1998). *Please understand me II, temperament, character, intelligence*. Del Mar, CA: Prometheus, Nemesis.

Offers Keirsey's view of how the temperaments differ in the intelligent roles they are most likely to develop. Each of us, he says, has four kinds of intelligence — tactical, logistical, diplomatic, strategic — though one of the four interests us far more than the others, and thus gets far more practice than the rest.

Myers, I.B. (1962). *Introduction to type*. Palo Alto, CA: Consulting Psychologists Press.

A comprehensive booklet describing the Myers-Briggs types and Jung's original type work.

Witkin, H., & Goodenough, D.R. (1981). *Cognitive styles: essence and origins*. New York: International Universities Press, Inc.

Covers the historical development of field dependence-independence and psychological differentiation, and the origins of cognitive styles. Summarizes and cites extensive research.

"KIDWATCHING" AND OTHER OBSERVATIONAL APPROACHES

Acpsta. D., et al. (September/October 1997). Home visits to middle-schoolers. *Schools in the middle*, 24-25.

Black, S. (June 1999). House calls: Visiting students' homes can help heal the breach between home and school. *American School Board Journal*, 34-36.

Comer, J.P., et al. (1999). *Child by child: The Comer process for change in education*. New York: Teachers College Press. Available: (800) 575-6566.

Goodman, Y. M. (1978). Kidwatching: An alternative to testing. *National Elementary School Principal*, 57(4), 41-45.

Goodman, Y. (1985). Kidwatching: Observing children in the classroom. In A. Jagger and M.T. Smith-Burke (Eds.), *Observing the language learner*. Newark, DE: International Reading Association.

Provides a thorough rationale for kidwatching as the major evaluation technique for early childhood teachers.

KOLB

Kolb, D.A. (1984). *Experiential learning: Experience as the source of learning and development*. Prentice-Hall, Inc., Englewood Cliffs, N.J.

Smith, D.M., & Kolb, D.A. (1986). *The user's guide for the learning-style inventory: A manual for teachers and trainers*. McBer & Company. Boston, MA.

MISCONCEPTIONS

Center for Science, Mathematics, and Engineering Education. (1997). Misconceptions as barriers to understanding science. In *Science Teaching Reconsidered: A Handbook*. Washington, D.C.: National Academy Press. Available: www.nap.edu/readingroom/books/str

VYGOTSKY

Doolittle, P. (1997). Vygotsky's Zone of Proximal Development as a theoretical foundation for cooperative learning. *Journal on Excellence in College Teaching*, 8(1), 83-103.

Vygotsky, L.S. (1962). *Thought and language*. Cambridge, MA: MIT Press. (Original work published in 1934)

Vygotsky, L.S. (1978). *Mind in society: The development of higher psychological processes*. Cambridge, MA: Harvard University Press.

Appendix C:
Selected References

Anderson, A. (March 2001). Tailoring assessment to student learning styles: A model for diverse populations. *AAHE Bulletin*. Available: www.aahe.org/bulletin/styles.htm

Armstrong, T. (1994). *Multiple intelligences in the classroom*. Alexandria, VA: Association for Supervision and Curriculum Development (ASCD).

Armstrong, T. (n.d.). *Multiple intelligences*. Available: www.thomasarmstrong.com/multiple_intelligences.htm

Black, S. (June 1999). House calls: Visiting students' homes can help heal the breach between home and school. *American School Board Journal*, 34-36.

Brewster, C., & Fager, J. (October 2000). Increasing student engagement and motivation: From time-on-task to homework. *By Request....* Portland, OR: NW Regional Educational Laboratory. Available: www.nwrel.org/request/oct00/index.html

Brualki, A. (September 1996). *Multiple intelligences: Gardner's theory.* Washington, D.C.: ERIC Clearinghouse on Assessment and Evaluation. (Digest EDO-TM-96-01). Available: http://ericae.net/digests/tm9601.htm

Bruner, J. Lecture 14. New Zealand: Department of Psychology, Massey University. Available: www.massey.ac.nz/~i75202/2001/lect14/lect1400.htm

Cambell, B. (Fall 1990). The research results of a multiple intelligences classroom. *On the Beam*, 11(1). Available: www.newhorizons.org/art_mireserch.html

Center for Adolescent Studies. (1996). Cultural diversity in the classrooms. *Teacher Talk*, 2(2). Available: http://education.indiana.edu/cas/tt/v2i2/cultural.html

Center for Applied Special Technology. (February 7, 2000). Ages and Stages. Available: www.nncc.org/Child.Dev/age.stage.page.html

Center for Science, Mathematics, and Engineering Education. (1997). Misconceptions as barriers to understanding science. In *Science Teaching Reconsidered: A Handbook*. Washington, D.C.: National Academy Press. Available: www.nap.edu/readingroom/books/str

Chirnside, D. Classroom Concepts: *Learning styles*. Available: www.classroomconcepts.co.nz/ls/lsindex.htm

Danielson, C. (1996). *Enhancing professional practice: A framework for teaching.* Alexandria, VA: Association for Supervision and Curriculum Development.

Dickenson, D. (ed.). (1998). Intelligence in seven steps: Howard Gardner. In *Creating the Future: Perspective on Educational Change.* Seattle, WA: New Horizons for Learning. Available: www.newhorizons.org/crfut_gardner.html

Educational Testing Service. (1999). *Letting students shine: Assessment to promote students in learning.* Princeton, NJ: ETS.

ETS. (2002). PATHWISE® *Minicourse for Teachers: Engaging students in learning.* Princeton, NJ: ETS.

_____. *Engaging kids.* Funderstanding.com. Available: www.funderstanding.com/engaging_kids.cfm

Felder, R.M. (n.d.). *Learning styles.* Raleigh, NC North Carolina State University. Available: www.2.ncsu.edu/unity/lockers/users/f/felder/public/Learning_Styles.html

_____. *Multiple intelligences: An overview* (The eight intelligences described). Teachervision.com: The Art of Teaching. Available: www.teachervision.com/lesson-plans/lesson-2173.html

Gardner, H. (1993). *Multiple intelligences: The theory in practice.* New York: Basic Books.

Giles, T. W. (1995). *A Piagetian view of learning styles.* ERIC ED, No. 404191.

Gill. H. (n.d.).. Kid Watching: A naturalistic assessment technique. An inservice presentation for K-6 teachers. Central Michigan University. Available: http://www.ehhs.cmich.edu/ins/kidart.perf

Golubtchik, B. (n.d.). *How to recognize learning styles.* Available: www.teachnet.org/ntol/howto/adjust/c13473,.htm

Gross Davis, B. (October 1993). Motivating students. *In Tools for Teaching.* San Francisco: Josse-Bass. Available: www.hcc.hawaii.edu/intranet/committees/FacDevCom/guidebk/teachtip/motiv.htm

Guild, P. (May 1994). The culture/learning style connection. *Educational Leadership*, 51(8). Available: www.ascd.org/readingroom/edlead/9405/guild.html

Guild, P.B. and Garger, S. (1998). *Marching to different drummers, 2nd edition.* Alexandria, VA: Association for Supervision and Curriculum Development.

Heineman, P.L. (1995). *Rita and Kenneth Dunn learning style instrument.* Available: www.personality-project.org/perproj/others/heineman/peps.htm

Hess, M.A. (March 26, 1999). *Teaching in mixed-ability classrooms: Teachers guide students down many paths to a common destination.* Wisconsin Education Counsel: Kids and Schools. Available: www.weac.org/kids/1998-99/march99/differ.htm

Hoffman, B. (n.d.). Piaget's developmental stages. *In Encyclopedia of Educational Psychology.* Available: http://coe.sdsu.edu/eet/Articles/piaget/index.htm

Honolulu Community College (HCC). (n.d.). Enhancing your teaching effectiveness. In *HCC Faculty Development Guidebook.* Available: www.hcc.hawaii.edu/intranet/committees/FacDevCom/guidebk/teachtip/enhance.htm

HCC. (n.d.). General principles of motivation. In *HCC Faculty Development Guidebook.* Available: www.hcc.hawaii.edu/intranet/committees/FacDevCom/guidebk/teachtip/motivate.htm

Holloway, J. (September 2000). Research link—Preparing teachers for differentiated instruction. *Educational Leadership*, 58(1). Available: http://www.ascd.org/readingroom/edlead/0009/holloway.html

Huitt, B. (June 1, 1997). The cognitive system. *Educational Psychology Interactive.* Valdosta, GA: Valdosta State University. Available: http://chiron.valdosta.edu/whuitt/col/cogsys/cogsys.html

Huitt, B. & Hummel, J. (January 1998). Cognitive development. *Educational Psychology Interactive.* Valdosta, GA: Valdosta State University. Available: http://pss.uvm.edu/pss162/learning_styles.html

Integrated New Technologies Into the Methods of Education (InTime). (n.d.). *Knowledge of Student Characteristics.* Available: www.intime.uni.edu/model/teacher/teac1summary.html

InTime. (n.d.). *Multicultural education.* Available:
www.intime.uni.edu/multiculture/index.htm

InTime. (n.d.). *Cooperative learning.* Available:
www.intime.uni.edu/coop_learning/index.htm

Kearsley, G. (n.d.). *Multiple intelligences (H. Gardner).* Available
http://tip.psychology.org/gardner.html

Kearsley, G. (n.d.). *Social development theory (L. Vygotsky).* Available:
http://tip.psychology.org/vygotsky.html

Kearsley, G. (n.d.). *Constructivist theory (J. Bruner).* Available:
http://tip.psychology.org/bruner.html

Lumsden, L. (1994). Student motivation to learn. Eugene, OR: ERIC
Clearinghouse on Educational Management. (Digest 92, ED370200).
Available: www.ed.gov/databases/ERIC_Digests/ed370200.html

McCombs, B.L. (2002). Understanding the keys to motivation to learn.
*Noteworthy Perspectives: Teaching to the Core — Reading, Writing, and
Mathematics.* Aurora, CO: Mid-continent Research for Education and
Learning. Available:
www.mcrel.org/products/noteworthy/noteworthy/barbaram.asp

Early Literacy Advisor. (n.d.). Developmentally appropriate practices in
teaching early literacy. Available:
www.mcrel.org/resources/literacy/ela/practices.asp

mdk12. (n.d.). *What have we learned about good instruction?* School
Improvement in Maryland. Available:
www.mdk12.org/practices/good_instruction/index.html

Meece, J. (1997). Improving student motivation: A guide for teachers and
school improvement teams. Washington, D.C: Office of Educational
Research and Improvement.

Mills, D.W. (January 2002). *Applying what we know: Student learning styles.*
Available: http://www.csrnet.org/csrnet/articles/student-learning-styles.html

National Board for Professional Teaching Standards. Available:
http://www.nbpts.org/

Eller, C. & Mulroy, M. (n.d.). Developmentally appropriate programming for school-age children. National Network for Child Care. Available: www.nncc.org/SACC/dev.approp.sac.html

National Council for Teachers of Mathematics. (2002). NCTM Professional Standards: (Professional Development Standard 3—Knowing Students as Learners of Mathematics). Available: http://standards.nctm.org/Previous/ProfStds/ProTeachM3.htm

North Central Regional Educational Laboratory. (n.d.). Pathways to School Improvement Web site. Available: www.ncrel.org/sdrs

Nicholl, T. *Vygotsky*. New Zealand: Department of Psychology, Massey University. Available: www.massey.ac.nz/~alock//virtual/trishvyg.htm

O'Connor, Terry. (n.d.). *Using learning styles to adapt technology for higher education.* Center for Teaching and Learning, Indiana State University. Web document Available: www.htctu.fhda.edu/prestools/ls/learning.html

Oesterreich, L. (1995). Ages & stages—Individual differences. In L. Oesterreich, B. Holt, & S. Karas, *Iowa family child care handbook*, [Pm 1541] 191-192. Ames, IA: Iowa State University Extension. Available: www.nncc.org/Child.Dev/ages.stages.indiv.dif.html

Otto, H. (May 2000). Multiple intelligences and meaningful learning. *Your Classroom* (article 4). TeacherHelp.com. Available: www.teacherhelp.com/article_archive/classroom_4.html

Parke, B.N. (December 1992). *Challenging gifted students in the regular classroom.* Arlington, VA: The Council for Exceptional Children. ERIC EC Digest No. E513.

————. *Piaget describes stages of cognitive development.* A Science Odyssey: People and Discoveries. Available: www.pbs.org/wgbh/aso/databank/entries/dh23pi.html

Perry, D. *Cognitive development theories* (Instructor notes for online course: Learning and Cognition in Education, Indiana State University School of Education, Bloomington, IN). Available: http://education.indiana.edu/~p540/webcourse/develop.html

Pettijohn, T. (1998). *Psychology: A ConnecText* (Fourth Ed.). Guilford, Conn.: McGraw-Hill Higher Education. Available: www.dushkin.com/text-data/catalog/0072929049.mhtml

Thorsheim, H. (1999). *Lev Vygotsky*. Northfield, Minnesota: Department of Psychology. Available: http://www.stolaf.edu/people/thorshm/vygotsky_wildflower_metaph.htm

Tomlinson, C.A. (1999). *The differentiated classroom: Responding to the needs of all learners*. ASCD: Alexandria, VA.

Tomlinson, T.M. (June 1992). Hard work and high expectations: Motivating students to learn. *Issues in Education*. U.S. Department of Education, Office of Educational Research and Improvement Programs for Improvement of Practice. Available: http://npin.org/library/pre1998/n00256/n00256.html

Vockell, E., & Schwartz, E. (n.d.). *Student misconceptions*. Available: http://education.calumet.purdue.edu/vockell/cai/Cai3/cai3misconception.htm

Voke, H. (February 2002). Motivating students to learn: Student engagement. *Infobrief* number 28. Available: www.ascd.readingroom/infobrief/200202_issue28.html

Wehrmann, K.S. (September 2000). Baby steps, a beginner's guide: The journey to a differentiated classroom starts with small steps. *Educational Leadership*, 58(1). Available: www.ascd.org/readingroom/edlead/0009/wehrmann.html

Woods, G. (n.d.). Reducing the dropout rate. NW Regional Education Laboratory: School Improvement Research Series. Available: www.nwrel.org/scpd/sirs/9/c017.html

Wyman, S.L. (1993). *How to respond to your culturally diverse student population*. Alexandria, VA: ASCD. Available: www.ascd.org/;readingroom/books/wyman93.html

Yang, Y.C. (2000). *Learning theories: Synthesis and comparison*. Available: http://expert.ics.purdue.edu/~yangyc/index/theory.html

APPENDIX D:
RELATED ACTIVITIES COMPLETION CHARTS

In order to track your progress through this minicourse, please note the dates you begin and complete each Related Activity in the following charts. Space is provided for additional activities that you complete to deepen your understanding of—and increase your skills in—the topics addressed in each chapter.

PART I RELATED ACTIVITIES	DATE BEGUN	DATE COMPLETED
1.1 MY MINICOURSE JOURNAL		
1.2 SELECTION OF STUDENTS FOR FOCUS		
1.3 KNOWLEDGE OF STUDENTS		
1.4 WHAT I LEARNED FROM OTHER RESOURCES — RELATED READING		
1.5 WHAT I LEARNED FROM OTHER RESOURCES — OTHER TEACHERS		

PART II RELATED ACTIVITIES	DATE BEGUN	DATE COMPLETED
2.1 MY MINICOURSE JOURNAL (A) DEVELOPMENTAL MODELS (B) LEARNING STYLE MODELS		
2.2 INFORMATION I WANT TO GATHER		
2.3 DESIGNING SURVEYS		
2.4 "KIDWATCHING"		
2.5 THE INVESTIGATIVE PROCESS — STEP 1: IDENTIFY		
2.6 THE INVESTIGATIVE PROCESS — STEP 2: GATHER INFORMATION		
2.7 WHAT I LEARNED FROM OTHER RESOURCES — OTHER TEACHERS		

Part III Related Activities	Date Begun	Date Completed
3.1 My Minicourse Journal		
3.2 Review of Differentiated Instruction		
3.3 Trying It Out—Using Differentiated Instruction		
3.4 Reflecting on Implementation		
3.5 The Investigative Process—Continue to Collect Information		

Part IV Related Activities	Date Begun	Date Completed
4.1 My Minicourse Journal		
4.2 (A) The Investigative Process—Step 3: Interpret Information (B) The Investigative Process—Step 4: Apply New Understanding (C) The Investigative Process—Step 5: Assess Progress and Plan Next Steps		
4.3 Investigative Process Narratives		

Part V Related Activities	Date Begun	Date Completed
5.1 My Minicourse Journal		
5.2 My Next Steps		

These materials are being sponsored by the Teaching and Learning Division of Educational Testing Service (ETS), a not for profit organization. One of the division's goals is to serve teachers' professional development needs by providing products and services that identify, assess, and advance good teaching from initial preparation through advanced practice.

Teaching and Learning
Division

Our mission is to help advance quality and equity in education by providing fair and valid assessments, research and related services. Our products and services measure knowledge and skills, promote learning and performance, and support education and professional development for all people worldwide.

WE WELCOME YOUR COMMENTS AND FEEDBACK.

Email address: professionaldevelopment@ets.org

Professional Development Group
Teaching and Learning Division
Educational Testing Service, MS 18-D
Princeton, New Jersey 08541

Notes

NOTES

NOTES

NOTES

NOTES

NOTES

NOTES